Freela

The Million-dollar Side-hustle That is Taking Over Africa

(Secret Tricks to Beat the Competition and Get Hired on Upwork)

Pedro Jackson

Published By **Bengion Cosalas**

Pedro Jackson

Freelancing: The Million-dollar Side-hustle That is Taking Over Africa (Secret Tricks to Beat the Competition and Get Hired on Upwork)

ISBN   978-0-9959962-5-0

Legal & Disclaimer

Table Of Contents

Chapter 1: The Psychology Of Freelancing

It can trigger emotions. A lot of freelancers are in a solitary environment and interact with their clients only through messages boards. Workspaces for freelancers are not as traditional workplaces. Contact with people in person is absent or infrequent. There's no one around who can bounce ideas off. Home demands can be relentlessly in your face. Clients who are demanding often challenge your endurance. This can leave you feeling exhausted. An elevated level of emotional intelligence, paired with a good level of communication, is essential for coping with the mental demands of freelance work on the internet.

Emotional Intelligence (EQ)

"Emotional Intelligence" is a concept developed by world-renowned psychologist Daniel Goleman. It's defined as "the capacity to be aware of, control, and express one's emotions, and to handle interpersonal relationships judiciously and empathetically." Individuals who have a high level of emotional intelligence perform successfully in conventional workplace settings and also in their lives. Consider a coworker or classmate who was successful with the majority, or even everyone you work with or in your class setting. There is a good chance that they had learned how to use emotional intelligence.

The lack of personal interaction in the workplace online is a challenge to implement the tenets that are the basis of a high level of emotional intelligence. Understanding the essential characteristics of emotional intelligence will enable you to connect to clients of any kind.

SelfAwareness

Your feelings are not the only thing that matter. You shouldn't allow them to control your life. Selfawareness means understanding how you're feeling and the reason for being the way that you feel as well as not imposing negativity onto others. This also means accepting your strengths while working on the shortcomings. Selfaware individuals know their own identity and strive to become the very best version of them.

SelfRegulation

Knowing how to handle your emotions and feelings is something. Controlling your emotions is a second. The people who are emotionally intelligent aren't prone to letting anger overwhelm them. They are also mindful of the decisions they make instead of acting in a hurry. They make decisions with the calm and rational view.

Motivation

Rarely does the flow of life happen effortlessly. Highly intelligent people are driven even when odds are stacked against their success. They realize that an assignment must be completed and will do whatever they can to make sure it is a achievement. The way they approach life results in highly efficient and successful individuals.

Empathy

Empathy is about being able to discern and comprehend other people's desires as well as their needs and views. The world isn't just about your own personal needs and wants. People are more likely to collaborate with those who are open and show genuine care of them. The ability to empathize is a major factor to build lasting connections.

Social Skills

The concept of teamwork is easy for those who are emotionally smart. People who are emotionally intelligent concentrate on the "we rather than" "I". They recognize that when other people excel, the entire group will be able to make progress towards successful outcomes. Effective communication is among their strength. They can also solve conflicts swiftly and effectively. Customers may ask them to collaborate with their group to accomplish their goals. The teamoriented approach, can be extremely beneficial for freelancers.

The ability to succeed as an online freelancer demands a high level of emotional IQ. Without this, you will not develop lasting relationships with your clients. In addition, you will not become a toprated freelancer since clients will not enjoy working with your. This is an important point because many freelancers who work online gain new customers through wordofmouth.

The initial step towards improving your intelligence emotional is to know the emotional quotient (EQ) score. Numerous websites provide the opportunity to take free EQ tests. An easy Google search will provide the list of the most popular tests. Try one to identify your weakest areas in

EQ. It is possible that you have identified them from the description given above, however conducting a test can give you an even more complete picture.

When you've identified weaknesses in your EQ After identifying your weak areas, you are able to implement one or two of the strategies listed below in your everyday routine. Building a strong EQ is a process that takes time and energy. Take a deliberate decision to apply the suggestions to your life on a regular basis until you've mastered the obstacle.

Say NO to Negativity

Our thoughts about negative things easily enter our mind. It is much more easy to concentrate on negative outcomes instead of the potential positive results of an event. What's important is to train your mind to place the positive spin on every scenario. Do not take it as a personal attack. Always be prepared with multiple choices to minimize the pain of rejection. Do not let fear stop your from taking bold steps.

Redirect Stress

Stress is part of every workplace. The ability to manage multiple projects is typical for freelancers who work online. In addition, you have to manage the many aspects of life to the mix, and your stress levels are likely to substantially grow. Training is an effective method to reduce the stress. The more relaxed you feel in your workout, the more secure you'll be. Set up a consistent, but basic exercise regimen and you'll be pleasantly surprised at your improved focus and willingness to accomplish work.

Set Boundaries

It is important to let the world know what you think. The needs of your client shouldn't be a hindrance to your personal safety and sanity. Be clear and respectful in communicating your values so there's no doubt regarding what you are about.

Failure isn't Final

The online freelance market isn't easy. It's difficult to do everything perfect with the first customer you meet. I've been freelance for more than four years, and still have moments of failing. It's crucial to recognize that failure doesn't mean the final word. It's just the beginning of your growth. Find out what you can gain from every experience and utilize this knowledge to improve your freelance skills.

These suggestions can assist you and your customers build a strong working partnership. The development of the capacity to have a higher EQ involves selfawareness and emotional regulation, selfregulation, motivation as well as social abilities. The ability of you to build these abilities is contingent in your ability to overcome negative thinking, redirect anxiety, establish boundaries and gain knowledge from your mistakes. Integrating both views will assist to effectively tackle another aspect of the mentality of freelancing online handling problematic customers.

Working with difficult clients

Every client is there seeking help in solving the issue. Clients aren't too worried with your personal problems The goal is simply to find an individual who will complete the task. That's why some clients can be extremely demanding and difficult to deal with. When this happens, it's crucial to establish an effective method for handling your interaction with clients. Following strategies can aid you to overcome this problem and ensure your reputation remains stellar.

Step One: Respond When Calm

Anger is among the most dangerous emotion. This triggers an impulsive response that can cause more harm than it does good. If a customer does things that make you feel uncomfortable then take a deep breath. Take a break for a short period of time when you must. Take some time to formulate a professional answer. It is important to never be angry and never respond.

Step Two: Be Proactive

What your client is looking for is the solution to the issue. It's possible that this is not communicated efficiently. Your job is to sort from the chaos and find the need. You should concentrate on solving the problem instead of the methods by how the customer gets your and gets under your.

Step Three: Produce Quality

Chapter 2: Views From Freelancers Who Are Practicing

Being the author of the book, I thought it essential to open the section by telling my personal background. My career as a freelancer began in 2013, with the launch of my website Christine Speaks. In the beginning, I wanted to have a place where my voice could be heard. I found the platform for freelancing Elance and later, UpWork and soon thereafter. My first time working as a freelancer, it was much like being on a mattress of thorns. It was a struggle to get anywhere. Bids after bids would always be denied. I have tried everything, from creating wellthoughtout proposals, bidding on the lowest cost as well as making appeals to my bid. The process was ineffective.

Then the light from Heaven appeared. Tatenda Sithole, owner of the website thepowerofwoman.net was seeking writers for empowerment of women content. I submitted a bid and was selected by her. It was a lot less than what I had would have liked, however it was the beginning I needed to launch my career. The relationship we established was one of professionalism lasting for six months. My confidence in her led to other opportunities for employment which led me to becoming an extremely rated freelancer through Elance.

The balance between online freelance and my fulltime employment has been very challenging. A few of the biggest issues I've faced are:

I am forced to decline work due to the pressures of my fulltime work

I am becoming extremely impatient due to my incessant fatigue

"I feel inadequate due to client"s' requirements

being in a position to not take on topquality jobs due to the time limitations

It's not possible to say with certainty that I've overcome all of the issues. However, what I can tell you but, is that in these past four years, I've grown enormously. I've come to terms with my temper and satisfy my customers' requirements. Also, I've learned to operate during the time I perform most effectively. My biggest lesson I've learned from this journey However, is the ability to learn from my mistakes.

My writing style isn't free of critique. I've come to accept the criticism, and then use it to enhance the way I write. What I have achieved is highquality writing that is tailored to my customers requirements. This has been my goal for years and will remain my aim.

A Freelancer who is married and has the birth of a baby

Shandean WilliamsReid

Business Plan Expert; Lifestyle Blogger; Social Media Manager

Website: shandeanwilliams.com

Twitter: @ShandeanWRBS

Shandean is driven to help companies grow. Her professional journey began working in the field of business analysts which was where she developed her writing abilities for business plans. When she was working fulltime she received requests from clients who needed the help of her writing skills for business plans. At the time, she didn't realize at that time the opportunities that were presented to her opened her up to the possibility of freelance work.

In 2016 she discovered she was expecting a baby. It was time to make a decision taken. Was she going to quit her job fulltime in order to look after her son? Should she contract someone to look after the child even though she was working at fulltime? The couple had numerous conversations with her husband on the subject during her pregnancy. Her answer was simple; they wanted no one else to look after their baby. Being at home, however did not mean that her husband was going to be sole breadwinner. The woman was already gifted with the capacity to write impressive business strategies. Therefore, she decided to turn her love for writing into an online freelancing company Shandean WilliamsReid Services.

Shandean started blogging casually in the year 2016. With time she began to find her niche in lifestyle blogs and was able to attract clients with her blog. Her business encompasses her strategy writing abilities and blog as well as social media management and content strategy expertise.

Being a mother to a baby implies that the child's needs have priority. This is Shandean's biggest challenge working as an independent freelancer. She must work around the schedule of her infant. The baby isn't able to be scheduled and isn't aware of when she has to be working. She is trying to finish most of what she must do while she is napping or her husband gets back after work. This is the great thing about the marriage: working together. With the help of her husband she can build her own brand, and accomplish her tasks that she has to do every day.

A Freelancer Pursuing a FullTime Freelancing Career

Phillip Taylor

Infographics and Typography Expert

Website: http://grtuts.com/

Design and art were always Phillip's top interests. Motivated by these interests that led him to quit the teaching profession he was in fulltime the year 2016 to explore a career in graphic design fully. He is a fan of the flexibility working for himself and making use of his talents. He describes the freelance world as difficult and lonely path.

Graphic design are not common in Jamaica in which Phillip is located. Thus, Phillip is without person to work with or discuss his experience with. Traditional workplaces provided an atmosphere where being in a room with people who were working provided enough incentive to finish his work effectively. Homework doesn't offer this kind of luxury. It's a solution to this: go to Jamaica's most recent space for entrepreneurs and freelancers called the Hub. It's a coworking area where users can lease workspaces as well as meeting rooms for business meetings. The environment is the freshness Phillip typically requires.

Phillip is also tapping into the potential of setting goals. He's discovered that if setting monthly and weekly objectives, he is able to accomplish greater and even manages to gain more clients. The more committed and determined his efforts, the more effective outcomes.

Freelancers are your average Joes. They're not millionaires living life filled with luxury. They're attempting to make money by doing something they enjoy as you do. No matter what your past or personal circumstances it is possible to make online freelance work for you. You'll need a stable internet connection, solid laptop, and the ability to define your goals are all that you require to successfully explore the online world of freelance. The other chapters in the book will equip the reader with stepbystep instructions that can assist you in becoming a desired freelancer.

Chapter 3: Creating Your Brand

Your image is the most important thing. The branding process helps customers instantly recognize the person you are and the values you represent. freelancers that achieve the highest degree of success are those with strong branding; they have brands that cause potential customers to take an extra look and think, "Wow! The person I'm looking for is exactly what I'm looking for!" Branding requires an commitment of both time and funds. This chapter concentrates on the key elements that make up the online brand for freelancing. Making these improvements is the best way to be an effective player on the freelancing market online.

Carving Out Your Niche

Before you get into the technicalities of developing your internet branding, you must be able to clearly define your service(s) you'll sell on the internet.

Freelancing online offers work that are in these areas:

IT and Programming

Graphic Design

VoiceOver Talent

Accounting and Bookkeeping

Administrative Support

Writing and Translation

Video Editing and Creation

Legal Support

Online Course Creation

Sound Mixing and Editing

The field you select is based on the area where your interest is. Every niche is a subcategory that's suitable to people who have different skills. It's up to you: How do you determine which niche is right for you?

Engaging in a field you aren't interested in is futile. It's a burden to work on. take a toll on you and devour the energy of your. The risk of failure is almost guaranteed. The field that you select is a true expression of what you enjoy doing. What is it that you are good in? What do you enjoy doing naturally? What is it that you are most interested in? Answering these questions can help you pinpoint your area of interest.

Some people but they don't have what the answer to these questions is. They're unaware of what they truly would like to accomplish and what they'd like to become. If you're among these folks, don't worry. These suggestions will assist you to discover what you're proficient at and determine where you're passionate.

Make A List

List the top five items that grab your attention. Create a second listing of your most valuable abilities. These lists with areas that are in close proximity can give you an indicator of where your interest is. In particular, take a look at these list of lists.

Interests

The world is your oyster

Reading good books

Writing

Aiding others

The guitar

Best Skills

Writing

Planning

Organizing

The main difference between these two lists is the writing. A person can turn into a content manager, who aids writers develop content for their business and also writes about music and travel. As a content strategist, she'll also be able develop the skills of planning and organizing. See if there is crosspollination between lists and consider practical methods in which these skills and interests could be utilized in online freelance.

Ask Your Friends

Your closest friends have the most intimate knowledge of you. You can ask them what you are good at. They may be able to reveal talents that you did not realize you were lacking.

Take an Online Personality Quiz

The profile of MyersBriggs personality type is one of the largest images of the people we are. The extensive research done to identify the traits of the 16 types of personality. After you've determined the personality type you're looking for and you've identified your personality type, it's time to review the wealth of data that is available about suitable jobs. Be patient.

You'll discover the field suitable for your needs and you'll be a rock star freelancer online.

Business Name

The purpose of branding is to make it easy for people to recognize. Prospective customers must be able associate an image with the products you're trying to promote. The name you choose to use will be the basis for every online activity. Many freelancers opt to make use of their personal names as business names. It is suggested that you design your name using keywords that are associated with your services.

To build a brand online, you must being as prominent as you can for search engines. A wellwritten and targeted content, as well as the use of keywords play a major role of how well your site ranks online. Thus, naming your business which is based on the correct keywords can do great. My company's name as an example is CEM Writing Services. I chose the word "writing services" in the title because this is exactly the services I offer. "Writing services" is also an extremely popular search term for my specific area of expertise on Google and other search engines.

A distinctive and interesting name is a great idea. A name that is unique and appealing can spark the interest of people and cause them to know more about the brand. If you're looking to go with a unique name, use words that are related to your field. The words you choose will eventually aid in creating an identity that is more wellknown.

Business Logo and Slogan

The logo of a business provides visuals for your business. This is what you need to use for all emails, social media accounts as well as your website. An elegant appearance is crucial. It isn't a good idea for your logo to appear like a extremely pixelated art piece.

Graphic designers with a high level of skill can be found on the following websites for freelance work:

99 Designs

Fiverr

UpWork

Dribbble

Behance Job

I've discovered extremely talented graphic designers through both Fiverr as well as UpWork. My logo was created by a freelancer via Fiverr.

The benefit of using a platform for freelancing for hiring professionals is that they have an abundance of individuals that you could select from. It is likely that you will find someone that has exactly the skills you're seeking.

Slogans can be as crucial as the logo or business name. They are concise and enticingly convey what customers can expect from you. These tips will assist you in

CEM
Writing Services
Creating stellar content

creating a message that is effective.

KISS for Perfection is an acronym with a lot of popularity that refers to keep it Simple stupid. The slogan should not contain more than eight words. The more concise the slogan longer, the more memorable it will be. My motto will be "Creating stellar content". The potential client gets confidence that the content that I create will be of the highest quality. State Farm

Insurance has one of the most memorable slogans I've ever come across. The slogan reads "Like a good neighbor, State Farm is there." It is clear that the insurance provider will be available whenever I require they. Make sure your message is simple to get the most effect.

Consistency is Key

The slogan you choose should be compatible to match your logo, corporate name and the values the brand represents. In other words, you shouldn't create an app using a tagline like "Writing content that sells" or a logo that is reminiscent of the appearance of a smartphone. Both aren't related and this slogan does not have anything in common with your company's brand.

Set Yourself Apart From the Competition

Take a moment to think about what sets your company from others. Include this information as a component of your brand's slogan. Apple's slogan "Think Different" is a typical example of slogan. Apple has, far more than other brand in the field of technology is known through its distinctiveness. Apple doesn't attempt to emulate any other company in the tech industry. They instead create items that help customers think different.

Remember Your Audience

The brand of an online freelancer is a global brand. The slogan you choose should reflect something everyone around the globe are able to relate to. If you've set out to limit the scope of your business to a specific geographic location, you'll be able to tailor your own slogan that is appropriate for the audience you're targeting. But, a phrase with more appeal to the masses is relevant and timeless in the event that you want to grow your enterprise in the future.

Business Email

There should be a clear distinction between professional and personal brands. The distinction between these two can be blurred within the online freelance world. An email address for business is the best way to create a distinct distinction between professional and personal names. GMail provides a function that lets users create email addresses that are linked to their business' domain name. The feature is available for a modest cost per month, but the service is worthwhile.

It is also possible to use the GMail domain if you like. What's important is to set up an email address for your business that every business email goes to. The email address you choose to use helps build a solid brand customers trust.

Website

Social media and websites constitute the basis of your online branding image. Prospective customers need access to a resource to find out more about the brand's reputation, browse your portfolio and establish contacts. Your site is that source. An effective website is equipped with these features.

Simple and Consistent Design

Each web page must have a common theme. The user shouldn't get confused with the design of your site each when he/she opens an online webpage.

MobileFriendly Design

The number of people who use mobile devices is higher more than ever. Every time you step out along the streets, you're likely to spot someone's attention on their tablet or phone display. The website you're creating should, consequently be able to be viewed on a variety of platforms. Every website page should load rapidly, feature an identical design and also be easy to use.

Use Content and Visuals Wisely

Content is among the primary components of a website. The content should not just be written well however, it must also contain appropriate keywords to boost the ranking of your website on search engines. Text blocks that are large in size can be an important deterrent to website users. The company Animoto claims that four times more consumers prefer to watch videos about products rather than reading about the product. The research carried out by SSRN shows that 65 percent of Americans are visuallyoriented.

Users want more images rather than reading texts. It's important to figure out an effective way of balancing the text and videos with suitable images while not compromising site load speeds. When you've found this equilibrium, your website will make your business stand out.

The majority of freelancers aren't web designers. Building a site from scratch will not be an choice. Other options are hiring a professional web designer or using the templates offered by a webbased builder. I chose the former because hiring a web designer can be very costly. The choice you make will depend on the amount you can afford.

There are many website builders available. One of the most wellknown website builders is WordPress. If you decide to use WordPress buy any template that catches your focus. The cost of the template grants users access to all the features, giving you more flexibility in changing it to the style you'd like. You can also buy a domain. Domain names are in the middle of your website's URL. The most common ones are .com, .edu, and .org. It is recommended to use the .com domain name is most appropriate choice since it's the most popular. But, you are able to be imaginative and create your own. However, a domain is an investment worth it.

I decided to go with SquareSpace due to the fact that I needed an attractive design for my website. Other platforms for building websites are:

Wix

Weebly

GoDaddy Website Builder

Make sure you do your homework and pick the right platform to meet your requirements.

Social Media Profiles

In 2016 in 2016, there was 2.3 billion active users of social media. Marketing on social media has exploded to connect with these people with a way that traditional marketing cannot. A freelancer's online brand isn't complete without a solid social presence on the internet. Social media enables you to connect with your customers and position yourself as an authority within your field. Facebook as well as Twitter are the two most important profiles to have. The Instagram app, Pinterest as well as SnapChat are ideal for freelancers working in a variety of visuallyrich media (photographers or videographers, marketers and photographers for example).).

Making a profile on social media is an aspect. The maintenance of it is a totally different ballgame. The social media account should not be dull. If it's not, your followers are likely to become bored. Making sure you update your profile frequently with interesting content, surveys video, interviews and other content related to your industry is essential. Plan a content plan for all of your social media profiles and adhere to the plan. An organized strategy helps keep your users engaged and can help to attract new customers.

Content Marketing

Social media accounts are tightly tied to strategies of content marketing. The most effective strategy to market content includes powerful images with striking and pertinent information. Infographics are among the most powerful forms of content, provides the ideal mix of pictures and words. Mass Planner states that "infographics are liked and shared on social media 3 times more than any other type of content." BuzzSumo recommends using images for content marketing by saying they "articles with an image once every 75100 words receive double the social media shares as articles with fewer images." The content marketing plan you choose to implement must therefore include the use of both images as well as content.

The choice of where you will publish the content is also important. The website you choose should include an online blog that you can create relevant content connected to your social media sites. If someone clicks the hyperlink on your social media pages you'll direct them to your web page. We hope they'll be impressed enough to visit your site, and eventually employ your services.

YouTube is a great source of content marketing. With YouTube's videos it is possible to make yourself an authority on your subject by giving videos that teach. Freelancers can earn over 75 percent of their customers by providing video tutorials. Customers are looking for solutions for their issues. The creation of "How To" tutorials related to the areas of concern within your field can help you stand out and attract new customers.

Putting It All Together

It is essential to establish your brand in order to be able to earn large sums of money online as a freelancer. The process of branding begins with selecting a name that is suitable as well as a slogan, logo and. A killer website follows. The website you create should be connected to professional profiles on social media you make for your company. In the end, it is important to employ every strategy for content marketing used to boost your business's reach. You won't get results overnight. As time passes and your business grows, you'll be able to see it grow into a profitable enterprise.

Chapter 4: Choosing The Right Platform

Freelancing platforms that are established offer many advantages for freelancers working online. Many freelancers have complaints about excessive service fees and the lengthy duration it takes to get access to funds through these platforms. The structure and organization that these platforms have to offer is far superior to their drawbacks. If you work on your own, you'll need to contend with

 ensuring that the payment you receive for the work you've done is secured

Finding ways to be able to access your cash efficiently even if you reside outside your home country of the United States, Canada and the UK

In the process of establishing a billing plan that is applicable to every client

Although tackling these issues isn't a daunting task but it is difficult and exhausting. In the end, you'll pay more the cost of money transfer that you pay for the service charges for platforms that allow freelancing. Clients who are honest may get more comfortable hiring your services with no total amount. We will go over strategies for combating these tactics in the following chapter. In the meantime, I am of the opinion that using online freelance platforms is the best option than attempting to do it on your own.

The last chapter discussed the creation of your own freelancer brand. Remember that you're your own brand regardless of your name that you use for your business. Better to make an individual profile for freelancers rather instead of a corporate profile. Customers generally prefer working on their own because it can be more personalised. It is possible to link the profile(s) that you set up using your platform of preference to your business's site and social media pages. But, if you'd rather to sign up as an agency and put your company's name on a freelance platform it is possible to do this also.

Several online freelancing platforms exist. The most popular platforms include:

UpWork

Freelancer

99 Designs

Fiverr

Toptal

Gigster

Folyo

Zirtual

Creative Market

Guru

PeoplePerHour

DemandMedia

iFreelance

Damongo

Smashing Jobs

Project4Hire

The choice of platform will depend on your preferences in terms of availability, features and preferences. I use UpWork and Fiverr. As these are two platforms that I'm most wellversed in which is why I can provide tips on how to become effective on both. If none of these platforms work for you, please consider doing your investigation on one of the sites mentioned above. The goal is to locate the best freelance platform for the needs of your specific situation.

Becoming a Top Rated Freelancer on UpWork

UpWork is among the top online marketplaces for freelancers. freelancers from all over the world with a variety of experiences and backgrounds can make profiles, and then apply for jobs that cover virtually every field. UpWork is the platform I use to search for new work. Here is a picture from my UpWork profile.

Let me be real. In the time that Elance and oDesk were merged, and then the change was transferred by UpWork and I was having issues adapting on the brand new system. It was as if I went to where I was. It was a constant source of frustration for several months. A few days ago, I made the decision there was no point in wasting time and that I had be able to take steps that would make the platform work for me. Within a few days, I started seeing positive results, and soon became the toprated freelancer through the platform. My approach was threefold.

Bid aggressively. It's not about hounding the customers or becoming annoying. You must be active with the site. Every month, you'll get 60 connects when you're on the basic plan. The goal was to bid the highest amount possible, until I ran out of connects available. I was only bidding on work I wanted to do and believed I could manage. In the end, I got the job of a potential client and have continued to receive job offers every since.

Rework my Profile Overview. My prior Profile Overview focused too much on my skills and experience. People who have read my profile would like to see what they could do to help them. This is why I changed the introduction of my outline to show the ways my skills in content marketing will benefit any customer.

Find jobs across other types of. UpWork offers freelancers the chance to bid for jobs of their choice, regardless of their field of work. I can bid on every job I can find that falls within the capabilities I have. This may mean searching for positions in the administrative and marketing category.

These are the methods that I have used and eventually led to my UpWork successful experience. The new freelancers who join the platform may require a little more direction. The tips below will assist you in creating a successful profile, submit your bids for work successfully, and be able to communicate with your clients.

Creating a Winning UpWork Profile

An UpWork profile is comprised of 9 key elements:

1.A profile picture

2.A catchy slogan

3.A video

4.An Overview

5.Work History and Feedback

6.Portfolio

7.Tests

8.Employment History

9.Education

Profile Picture

Pictures speak volumes. The image you present on your UpWork profile picture will be your professional brand image to all the world. Photofeeler conducted an investigation in 2014 to discover the most important features to consider when creating the perfect profile picture. The results are here.

Show Your Eyes

The people who admire you want to look into your eyes. Eyes that are blocked make you appear not trustworthy and are difficult to relate with. It's also acceptable to slightly squint your eyes. Photofeeler says the following "wide open eyes denote fear, whereas slightly squinted eyes portray comfort and confidence."

Showcase Your Jawline

An outline of shadows that outlines the entirety of your jaw will make it appear more skilled as well as likable and persuasive.

Smile

There's nothing more effective at making an individual appear more friendly more than a real smile. Your teeth ought to be apparent however, your mouth should not appear to be shut in an open smile.

Dress Formally

Dress code formality enhances a customer's impression of your professionalism and authority.

Avoid Extreme Editing

A photograph that's too dark can make you less appealing to people. Also, having a higher hue doesn't earn your photo any points. Keep your photo as natural as possible.

The tips above can be applied in any professional image used for your web branding. Psychological Science states that it is around 40 milliseconds to allow us to form conclusions about a person by looking at their pictures. They aren't any different. Create a great impression with these suggestions to take an image that is professional and appealing.

Slogan

I've noticed that the UpWork slogan should be treated differently than the slogan of your business. When it comes to the UpWork slogan, you can use keywords to reign the day. The slogan I use is essentially a list of the services I provide. The clients are in a position to know whether I offer the service they require.

A Video

Videos will give you a competitive edge over the competition as are very few UpWork freelancers utilize this option. In the preceding section, the majority of Americans use visual content. Americans aren't the only group, but this statistic provides a broad view of the significance of content that is visual.

The video needs to describe the person you are, your work you're doing, as well as the benefits you could provide to your clients. This is the ideal opportunity for prospective clients to find out more about your company and build a relationship with you before even making contact. Customers who are interested in engaging with them. Offer them the chance.

The Overview

The picture of your profile, the slogan and even your video will surely make your prospective clients hungry. The summary is what draws their attention and assists to make the final choice on whether to hire your company. A great overview should include these elements:

A clear understanding of what you can do to help the client.

Tell us about your success and the your relevant credentials

Your commitment to the customer

Being a writer, I prefer this data to be written into paragraphs. The format of my outline on this page. An effective overview of your work is crucial element to attracting attention and convincing someone to work with your services.

Work History and Feedback

It's the part of your profile which has the most control over. It highlights your projects that you've accomplished and the customer's comments regarding the work you've accomplished. Giving clients highquality work and providing them with a pleasant service should be the objective. When you achieve this you will be more likely to give positive reviews, both in private and public.

UpWork customers are able to leave two kinds of feedback for freelancers: both public and private. Your public feedback is a score from 5 to 5. It is based on the your work quality, abilities available, the capability to meet deadlines, collaboration, and communication. Customers give you a score five out of five for each of the criteria. They then add up the scores for a overall star rating. The public feedback section also offers the option to compose a letter detailing their experiences with you.

Private feedback is visible only to the user. The feedback doesn't show up on your profile but it's one of the main factors that affect your job success score. I've discovered that some clients give excellent feedback in public forums however, they leave very little personal feedback. This is why my Job Performance score drops. Feedback from private sources allows clients to rate you in a scale of 10 which reflects the likelihood they have likely to be rehiring you. Your goal is to provide your customer with the most pleasant experience so that he or gets a score that is as close to a 10 as feasible.

The Portfolio

Your portfolio showcases your work. The client wants proof of what you're competent at. This is particularly true for freelancers who work in the field of graphic design. Portfolios are essential regardless of the field you work in. Make a stunning portfolio utilizing your most impressive works. Your portfolio should help to make yourself stand out as an expert in your area. Provide links to previous jobs and a brief description of the way your work has helped resolve the client's issue.

Tests

UpWork has a wide range of tests for free. Successfully passing these tests gives credibility to your profile. Customers use these tests, your application, the comments received from clients as well as your portfolio, to decide which candidate is the best candidate to be hired. They are more important on prospective clients than other tests. However, scoring high at them will boost your reputation.

Employment History and Education

Education and employment history are located on the bottom the profile. They are, therefore, the only details that clients see. A majority of customers don't scroll to see all the details. Instead, they concentrate only on the things that immediately pop into their focus: your profile image the slogan, your overview, scores for job performance, your work history as well as feedback.

Complete this part of your personal information, however it is essential to create a complete and accurate profile. This section also confirms that you are able to hold an occupation and hold credentials or degrees that are relevant. Be sure to complete this form with accurate and pertinent details.

Applying for Jobs

The creation of a compelling profile is just one step of the process. Your real test will be the ability you have to craft compelling proposals that will convince customers to employ them. The proposals you write should be clear and correct in grammatical terms. There's nothing more uncomfortable than looking at a proposal that's or is strewn with grammar errors or not properly structured. The proposal should answer the most fundamental question that clients need to know: how do you assist me in solving my issue? The answer to this question isn't creating a lengthy essay about your qualifications and experience. It's more about tailoring every proposal to address issues outlined in your job description.

In Up Work's proposal, there is an email cover letter, as well as any other questions that clients can choose to inquire about. Certain clients do not make use of the extra questions feature. I'm using UpWork for both my client as well as a freelancer. Below's screenshot shows the job I just put up on UpWork. I've highlighted important aspects in my post that the majority of applicants didn't realize.

A majority of job ads regardless of length, contain the following three parts that are: a problem and specific details about the job and specific guidelines to make the proposal. Customers also have the opportunity to address specific questions of the freelancer. They respond to a job advertisement by composing the cover letter as well as answering the other questions clients could ask about within the job advertisement.

The initial thing be focusing on is your cover letter. Every customer has a problem area; an issue one cannot resolve on their own. The cover letter you write should be addressing the issue. It must be the first item you see when reviewing the description of your position. When you've identified the problem think about strategies you can employ to address the issue. This information must appear in the initial paragraph of your letter. The reason I was unhappy was that I'd had a terrible encounter with the freelancer who created the initial logo. I was in need of an expert to develop a logo that accurately represented the company within 24 hours.

Take note of the details of the job as well as any additional instructions the customer could give to you regarding your proposal. I suggested that all applicants must include "absolutely delicious" at the beginning of their proposal to show that they have completed the job posting in its entirety. Reviewing the complete job posting was vital because it outlined everything I required the freelancer to complete to accomplish the task. Any freelancer who didn't comply were instantly rejected. Make sure that the cover letter follows the guidelines within the description of your job. Also, it assures the client you are fully aware of what is needed.

The cover letter you write could be finished in the first paragraph. In the end, you've answered the customer's concerns. Additionally, you improve chances of getting employed if the proposal you submit is among the first things a potential client is exposed to. The faster you can submit your proposal an application, the greater chance of being hired. You can also write another paragraph to link your skills and experiences to the requirements of the job. One thing to remember however is to not sell yourself short. Make sure to include only enough details in the paragraph that you can show your client that you've had similar issues solved before or have the necessary skills to resolve the issue. Make sure to end your note with a comma or two that invites the reader to contact you. The letter invites the reader to establish a relationship. Connections can help make the sale.

Take note of any additional concerns the applicant might have in the job ad. The questions will differ from one job to another. Be sure to read the question thoroughly and make sure you describe your responses. Make sure you don't use one word answers. An introductory sentence or two could make you stand out from your opponents.

It is important to know the bid amounts in the event that a potential client is thinking about hiring your company. Every job advertisement has an accompanying budget. The client sets these budgets with reasons. Any freelancer who bids more than the limit of their budget typically are rejected instantly. Make sure you bid within the cap on budget. If you think you are being unfairly charged for the work be sure to explain why when the client calls you. Then, begin talks at that point. In order to convince clients to consider your offer is the main aspect.

Let's look at the 3 initial ideas I've received to fill my Logo Design job post.

The proposals and the portfolio samples attached to them did me any favors. Another proposal totally didn't respond to my request that it include the phrases "absolutely delicious". The freelancer isn't paying close attention to the details, which is an essential skill to this position. The proposals were not able to adequately met my needs. The experience is great, however I wanted an expert who could truly comprehend the best way to convey a company's values in an image. I didn't see how they can do it.

This sample offers a peek at how a client is thinking. Certain clients are more particular, but a client who has a thorough job description like mine is likely to be very selective. Offer the prospective client an incentive to choose your company.

My friend excels as a software engineer. He's not been able to make much progress on UpWork but this is because the company claims Indians have always won the bidding battle. In reality, there cannot be a surefire method for getting a client to sign up. You can, however, make every effort to impress your client by the proposal. I'm betting that if you structured your proposals in a way that they are solving the client's issues and showing how his expertise can solve their problem then he'd get a job. In addition, if he offered at the cheapest price the client is willing to accept the chance to get an employment opportunity to boost his UpWork professional career. It's all it takes is one task.

Maintaining Top Rated Status

Being a toprated freelancer through UpWork is an incredible achievement. The benefits of the platform are designed to aiding freelancers to find jobs through increased exposure. Maintaining your membership However, it's not quite as simple as you think. This was something I had to learn by trial and error. After a few months of writing and publishing the eBook My JSS (JSS) fell to the low of 88 percent (see the below screenshot).

I was shocked! My mind was flooded with thoughts of how everything I had put into was in vain. Perhaps it was due to bad personal feedback received from my customers? It didn't make sense to me from my interaction with my clients, and also the glowing public reviews that they'd left. I tried for hours to find the source of the issue. Then it occurred to me the fact that I'd cancelled around four jobs during that time. Reasons for cancelling included:

1. The client was not responsive. I was hired by this person to design an eBook on his life. However, he hadn't given me all the necessary information to make the ebook. Every week, he'd tell me that he'd get the book's content at the time the week was over. This never took place. I considered it an unnecessary waste of time, and decided to cancel the project.

2. The jobs I wasn't able to finish due to my arduous work or my lack of enthusiasm.

The experience has taught me not to cancel jobs via UpWork. Job cancellations can have a significant impact on the quality of your JSS. It is necessary to have a JSS that is at least 90 percent and also be a toprated freelancer for at minimum 13 weeks out of 16 weeks to qualify for UpWork's top Rated Program. Do not accept a task which you are unsure you will not be able to finish because of the profit or the pressure of an earlier customer. Make sure you are truthful about yourself. You'll have a variety of chances to discuss terms, or even quit a work before you accept an invitation.

Putting it All Together

To become a toprated Freelancer with UpWork is a matter of having an active profile, an extensive and properly compiled profile, the capability to create winning proposals as well as completing projects successfully, without having to cancel. If you can master these three skills, you'll be on the right track towards the top of the heap. If you have any questions, please feel free to contact me via my website cemwritingservices.com.

Chapter 5: Creating A Winning Fiverr Profile

Fiverr was founded with a platform for freelancers to sell gigs for five dollars. All the services offered on the website were only five dollars. The freelancer could provide gigs with extras for extra income

However, the basic idea was that no gig could be over 5 dollars. It's been changed. freelancers can now provide gigs at all price points. Additionally, they can bundle their services into packages to accommodate each job. This has helped make the business more profitable for a lot of freelancers.

Perhaps you've looked at that sentence and been completely lost. You're brand new to the world of technology which is why you're not even aware what a gig actually is. The gigs are basically tilelike tiles which showcase your offerings. Contrary to UpWork which requires you to send proposals to be chosen, customers on Fiverr will come to your. Customers can browse the various categories of work available on the website or look up the specific product they are looking for. Fiverr offers gigs across these niches:

Graphics and Design

Digital Marketing

Writing and Translation

Video and Animation

Music and Audio

Programming and Tech

Advertising

Business

Fun and Lifestyle

If a customer is able to locate the perfect service the client will then be able to choose among the many jobs that are available.

Excellent gigs and effective promotion strategies are essential to Fiverr successful. An image from my Fiverr profile can be found below.

My experience on this platform has been due to wellplanned gigs, the ability to deliver topquality work, as well as promotion on social media.

Creating the Best Gigs

The following elements are essential to the success of a show:

1.The gig's image and the title

2.Choosing the correct class

3.Packages

4.Description of the Gig

5.Tags

The Gig Image and Title

Fiverr is a visually appealing site that is very visual. It is organized into categories, and then advertised with a prominent picture and gig's title. I strongly believe that an attractive image for your gig which describes your service and grabs the attention of your client. The screenshot from my highest seller gigs on Fiverr can be seen below.

I've utilized the image from my gig to show off my personal brand. The tagline of my company and the logo appear prominently. An image with professional quality that is in line with the guidelines that are discussed in the chapter 4 is important in the picture. In addition, I've listed the services I provide so customers can quickly determine whether the services I provide are the service they require. The way you structure your gig's image this manner will allow you to draw a customer's attention.

Relevant keywords are crucial to the title of your gig. Every Fiverr gig begins by saying "I I ...". The company wants you to concisely describe what you'll do to help your customer. This is an opportunity to show off your most impressive skills. Use adjectives to add impact to your messages. My job's name will be "I will write amazing website content." Customers realize that they'll get website content but it's not a dry, boring web information. It's the kind of content that's guaranteed to be extraordinary.

Choosing the Right Category

The gigs must be as relevant as is possible. A proper placement of categories can help increase relevance. The kind of category you pick depends on the area your offerings are categorized under. If you're offering app development, for example it's best to put your gig(s) within the category of Programming and Technology. If not, clients may not be able to locate the gig.

Packages

Fiverr has introduced a package option in the year 2016. This feature lets freelancers group their services in order that they are able to provide more worth for their customers. Imagine it as the silver, gold and platinum reward program. The higher you go in the program, the greater amount you will have to spend on highend services. In the same way, higher package prices are higher however, they also offer clients additional options. Fiverr states that gigs using packages have higher success than gigs without.

Take a look at the best way to organize your services into categories. What is the amount of work you willing to put in and how much cash? What is the best way to structure what you provide for each of your packages in order to get reasonable value, without looking too expensive? These questions will allow you to create packages that will be a success.

Gig Description

The gig's title, image and the packages are what draw customers toward the lure. The description of your gig is what attracts them. A fantastic description for your gig is flawlessly written, wellstructured and clearly outlines the benefits you offer to your clients. Keywords relating to your offerings are best placed strategically throughout the description. This can help increase your position in the Fiverr search engine. Make sure you've answered these questions within the description of your gig

1.What are the contents of this contract?

2.What is it that makes your company unique?

3.How do you think your expertise can contribute value?

One of the main problems I've encountered concerning Fiverr is that customers are able to place orders without contacting. The sudden order has disrupted my schedule previously. So, I've ensured that an emphasis on that you must contact me before putting orders is included on both the top and in the final description of gig.

Tags

Tags are a great way to boost the search engine rankings through Fiverr. These tags won't always place your business on the top or second page based on the competition within your area of expertise. But, they can help some in helping prospective clients discover your business. Tags are basically relevant keywords that can be typed into the search engines. Consider all the possible keywords for your services included in your project. Fiverr lets you make use of up to five. Make use of all the options when you are able to.

By creating a quality gig you're one step closer your Fiverr dream of success. You are able to create the number of gigs you'd like. However, I recommend creating just 2 or 3 gigs. Even though I've had six gigs in my Fiverr profile, only two have been successful. In this situation.

Promotion of your gig is what is the most important factor that determines its success. If you can attract more people towards your page and the higher visibility it will appear in the search results of Fiverr's engine. A higher visibility will increase the probability of receiving orders. The more orders you receive, the greater your revenue. Twitter, Linked In groups as well as Facebook groups have been among the methods I've utilized to market my gigs. Making use of Twitter hash tag that include my website's URL has lead to several customers getting in touch with my profile. posting statuses or discussions in commercial and marketingrelated Linked In and Facebook groups is also helping me to be recognized. It's important to note that these aren't the only ones you can make use of. Make sure you research the best platforms and promote the most you are able to.

Promotions that are wellplanned and with a strong working ethic will guarantee Fiverr successful growth. Combine these factors with welldesigned jobs and you'll be a Level 2 seller quickly. The following chapter is focused on creating an online freelance business beyond freelancing platforms. Following this chapter, you'll be able to identify the method which best meets your objectives.

Establishing an Independent Freelancing Business

Options. The world of online freelance has lots of options. It is possible to work solely from a platform for freelancing or solely from your own. I've observed that mixing these two methods is the well. Combining both strategies helps create longlasting clients and also get new clients. This chapter will focus on the strategies which can be employed to build a profitable freelancebased business.

Billing Clients

One of the issues that freelancers are faced with is figuring out which rates are the best for clients to pay. The freelancers who work online are usually regarded as the type of person who is employed at a low price to receive top quality tasks completed. Make sure you know your worth. If you're just starting in the business and don't have an established track record, you shouldn't be expected to offer premium rates. Find out the standard costs for your expertise and skills, and make use of this information to create competitive pricing. The prices shouldn't be excessive or excessively low. A price that is too low indicates you're trying to hard or your client isn't getting the level of service that the client wants. If you're too high, it means that you're overestimating your capabilities in particular if you're new freelancer. Choose a level that is comfortable for you.

Hourly rates tend to perform better than fixed prices. Customers will only be charged according to the amount of time that you've given to the project. This makes it easier to bill. A variety of time trackers are readily available, the ones that are most highly evaluated including Clockodo, Hubstaff, TMetric Time Tracker and Toggl. Each application comes with the ability to track time. When you've enabled the time tracker feature, pictures are recorded of your actions and a stop watch tracks the time. Customers will therefore know that you've done your work, and you'll be able to issue invoices for the number of time you worked.

Fixed rate work has its position. Within my area of expertise, which is the field of content marketing, it's easy to determine an affordable price for the writing of an article or a book. The most important thing is having the same price but with pertinent additions that apply to the entire range of jobs. In my case, for instance, my basic cost for writing a 500 word piece is 10 dollars. But, if the client needs keyword research as well as the creation of an SEO article, my price can be raised to between $20 and $25. Certain jobs that aren't included in my pricing guidelines, but using a standard to work with helps determine the best pricing.

Payment Method

One of the greatest problems I encountered while trying to start a business of my own was figuring out the most effective method of payment. My home is in Jamaica. This means that payment systems like PayPal can't be easily accessible for me. If you're within a location that's which is covered by PayPal then you should use PayPal. It can make invoicing and accepting payments ten times more simple. The fees for PayPal can be extremely high, especially when moving funds from to PayPal account to an account at a bank. The tools offered by the company streamline the process, and provide customers with a confidence in their confidence.

Accounts at banks are also viable payments options. Clients can request to transfer funds into your local bank account, if they are also residents of your own country. Avoid this approach when they are outside your own country. It's enough to cause you to die.

Creating Invoices

Deciding when you should send an invoice is essential. Being a freelancer on a different platform, you won't benefit from security of payments or even a person for mediation with clients. To ensure your security, you should have the following:

1.a agreement that you and the customer must sign stating the nature of work, an agreement regarding payments terms and late payment policies, and the agreed payment method.

2.a down payment which covers some portion of the project. This down payment is proportional to the cost of the project and must be organized in increments. As an example, you might declare that a 50% down payment is necessary for jobs less than $30. You could also require and a 30 percent down on jobs that range from $31 to $200, and a 25 percent down payment for jobs that exceed $200. Don't start work until you've received your down amount.

After you've implemented these two protections, you'll be able to make an invoice. PayPal provides an invoice tool which works flawlessly. It is easy to make invoices and then send invoices to your clients. PayPal bundles your invoices paid together and permits you to issue reminders to customers who aren't paying.

If PayPal doesn't suit your needs You can try Invoiced. Invoiced is an invoice maker that lets users to design appealing and practical invoices. It is possible to download each invoice and store them in your PC. The downloaded invoices are able to be emailed to customers. Be sure to have an invoice for every job. This is essential for keeping track of the work and allows you to maintain track of who's been paid and who's not.

Collecting PastDue Invoices

Always take an active rather than reacting to everything that happens in your the world. Receiving payment from customers isn't the exception. When you've completed the work make sure you send a simple note to remind the client of their payment. The message should contain your statement that you've done the task and your final payment due on X date. Make sure to remind the client about your policy regarding late payments.

Any freelancer working on their own must use the AR managing app. They help manage every aspect of accounts receivable parts of your business. The most wellknown

AR management applications is FG Receivables Manager. It helps you categorize invoices in order to identify those that are due to the due date, and the ones that are past due.

Do not allow too long for the overdue payment. The client should be informed immediately when an invoice has been due. Your email should contain:

1.Details of correspondence from the beginning.

2.The equivalent invoice.

3.A reminding of the payment due date.

Spend the time to figure the root of the client's indebtedness. It is essential to show empathy. The situation of each client is different, and you may be able to come up with plans for paying in times that you are facing extreme financial difficulties. It is essential to be sure to keep track on your bills. Do not let any invoice slip away.

Boosting Productivity

The online freelance market requires an ardent dedication to work and a determination to complete tasks. Giving in to the temptation to put off work is not difficult. There is nothing worth having that's simple. The reason for procrastination is usually the inability to work and being overwhelmed, or simply a lack of motivation. There are tools for productivity which you can utilize to improve your performance to get more work done. There are strategies you could use to boost your enthusiasm and eliminate the effects of any laziness. Let's talk about them.

Asana as well as Google Docs are two tools to help you plan and work effectively on your tasks. Your clients can be able to give you tasks using either of the platforms. Tasks can be split into smaller tasks. Each job can be checked off when it's finished. Customers can leave their feedback and comments to ensure you can complete your work in the way you want. Check out these tools to see how they could simplify your work.

Wunderlist has been a great help to maintain my focus. It permits you to make Todo lists. The lists can be organized by category and then each task is checked off when it is complete. I like separating my work and then hearing the "ping" sound whenever something is ticked off on the list. It's a great feeling knowing that I've accomplished an item accomplished.

It is essential to rest. The best way to overcome being overwhelmed and drained of energy is taking a break. Have your time to have some "me time". Make time to reflect and reflect on the things you've been thinking about. You should make sure there's a of the days during the week you don't work for a rest and the time with your family. This will allow to approach every project from a different perspective, so you'll be able to produce topquality results.

Communication

I've sat on the opposite one side as a customer. One thing which I'm aware of as being severely missing for many freelancers is the ability to communicate. Communication is what connects everything. A lack of communication results in clients who are unhappy and isn't likely to recommend your business to friends. The lack of communication can be more damaging.

I'd like to share some of my latest experience with you. I hired a freelancer create a logo for a business of a friend's (the identical logo I described in my UpWork example of a job in chapter 5.). The concept was excellent however she didn't bother to incorporate the colors I requested and had omitted the tagline completely. The design was also not sent as an image that was printready. I notified her. A couple of days later, I was not receiving a response, even though I had asked the person to get in touch since my friend required an image to design the promotional materials. All she had to do was contact. If she had difficulties, I would've agreed to work together to complete work done within reasonable time. The only thing she had to do was inform me. However, I did not hear anything. This freelancer is one I won't repeat using. I wouldn't suggest her to potential clients.

Communication that is poor can give your business a negative image. It's not something you want to do. Always reply to clients' needs within 12 to 24 hours. The whole day's time is a bit much. Don't let it extend longer than 24 hours unless you've previously indicated to your client that you will not be available for a prolonged time.

Communication that is misinterpreted is a major issue that online freelancers face. Customers aren't able see your nonverbal communications or the voice you speak. They are relying on the words that you write. Thus, any message you type is as professional as feasible. Don't leave anything to chance. Try to be as precise as possible without appearing rude or blunt. Take it in your perspective as a client. Do you see any problems regarding the content?

Being a freelancer who is independent on a freelance platform isn't easy. However, with proper prices, payment methods as well as a strong work ethic and transparency, you can build an effective company. It's in your hands.

Chapter 6: Using Content Marketing To Promote Your Brand

Marketing content is my child as well as my love of writing and also my first passion. I frequently talk about it as I am passionate about writing. Writing articles, blogs and funny blog posts are powerful methods of marketing content that assist in promoting your brand. There are many ways to market your content but three are those that I believe are the most effective for freelancers.

This chapter is focused on writing blog posts and articles. Blogs are an essential element of your site. If the blog's content is written using the most effective SEO techniques it will attract visitors to your site that will eventually become paying customers. Blog content can also boost the relevance of your site and permit users to utilize words that can boost the page's rankings on the search engines. But, writing well can't be a standalone notion. Management of your content is vital in keeping your readers interested. Blending visual content like videos and images is essential as well.

Tips for Writing Good Content

Five characteristics of an excellent article:

1.A Catchy Title

2.Headings which make skimming the text simple

3.Relevancy

4.Writing that is appealing to the people who are the intended recipients.

5.Stunning pictures that relate to the topic

A Catchy Title

The title and image are among the first elements viewers will see. They should have a very precise title. Examples "5 Terrible Mistakes to Avoid When Saving" is much more precise as "How to Save". Make use of powerful words and make sure that the purpose of the piece gives is obvious. As an example "12 Killer Lifehack Tips from Leaders Who Win at Success" is far superior than "Tips for Living a Successful Life".

The titles that include that there is a list of contents are also more effective than titles with no list. In this case, someone who reads "12 Killer Lifehack Tips from Leaders Who Win at Success" is likely to find 12 strategies he could use to achieve success. This is a huge benefit to the article and increases more likely to be shared with others.

The length of titles should not exceed 70 characters. Anything that is longer than that is likely to be rejected by the search engines. A shorter and punchier title is typically better since they are easier to read for a reader.

Relevant keywords need to be included in the title. Create an account on Google AdWords account and use their Keyword

Planner tool to search for terms that are relevant to the subject. Keywords that have a large number of searches should be included in your titles since they can make your content more noticeable.

In addition, the title are required to be displayed in the featured image of your article. The image featured in your article must be professional and relevant to the topic discussed in your article. Snappa is a great instrument for creating featured photos and posts on social media. This is perfect for folks like me, who don't have graphic design skills and zero design expertise. Simple to work with templates and pictures are all there. It's easy to find something that you would like.

Remember your Audience

After you've found your title and the featured image, you're now ready to start writing the text. The content you write should be designed with the audience at heart. Take note of their language as well as their needs. Avoid using jargon that they don't connect to. Use a style that is appealing to them and not make off them. The writing is useless without the support of an public audience.

Relevant Content

The content you write about should be related to the subject matter you're writing about. The reader should not click the article on cupcakes in the case of printing company. Every piece of content you publish should reflect the message of your company. Unrelated content can confuse readers and does not add value to the marketing efforts you run. Content must also be valuable for the user It should also be something that readers can take away and make you appear as a specialist in your field.

Visuals

The image featured is not the only picture you can include in your article. Studies have shown that posts with more photos are more popular with readers. Avoid overflowing your content with photos, but figure out ways to weave important images within the text.

They are also an excellent way to increase the interest of an audience. MWP reports the fact that 55% the population go online to watch video each day. Furthermore, EyeView reports that "including video in a landing page can increase conversion by 80%." Many people enjoy videos. Add videos in the first paragraph of your content and you'll be certain to experience the increase in clickthrough rate.

Content Management

The art of writing good content is one thing. Getting customers to read the content is an entirely different thing. Content management can help to ensure that you are writing consistently, to ensure that the interest of your business is sustained. One of the hardest aspect of blogging is the fact that you have to write posts regularly enough. The life gets busy and there are times when you aren't inspired.

Writing in bulk is a option to manage the number of blog posts. If you're able, compose enough posts to fill your blog's needs for a month. If you plan to publish every week say, compose four posts at once. Every article you write is able to be scheduled on any time you want and then you are able to return to revise it at any point. Your readers must be able to trust your company's reputation for consistently useful, and pertinent content.

Content Management Systems (CMS) help content marketers manage digital content. The software lets you make content, and then publish it on every website and blog websites you are able to access. The top CMS software includes:

Contentful

Buzzsprout

WordPress

Wild Apricot

ClubRunner

Christine Speaks, my blog Christine Speaks Christine Speaks, was built by using WordPress and I've thoroughly been enjoying using the site. It's extremely simple to use, and includes an app to allow me to review my posts on the go. When I am struck with a surge of creativity, I create an article and then schedule it to publish. Every article is linked directly to my personal social media accounts. Thus, whenever the posts are published, they will also are posted as posts on my personal social media accounts.

My site also includes blog features that provide similar features to WordPress. Be sure that your website is equipped with blogs that have the CMS features listed. It will help you save a lot of effort and time.

Blogs are a must for freelancers working on the internet. Blogs can increase the chances that your site will rank higher on search results if you use the appropriate keywords. They also improve engagement as well as the potential to create leads of a highquality to your company. Use the guidelines in this chapter to write highquality articles and directing your content, and you'll have a solid blog.

Using Social Media and PayPerClick Advertising to Promote Your Brand

Content marketing, social media and paidperclick advertisements operate in conjunction. Social media profiles are required to provide regular and consistent content. The major social media platforms offer payperclick (PPC) advertisements. This chapter will discuss how to use each of these marketing techniques to market your company through Facebook as well as Twitter.

Marketing on social media starts with picking the best platform. In Chapter 3, I explained that the platform you pick is contingent on the type of services you provide. Instagram, for example, is a great choice for photographers, graphic designers as well as video producers as well as editors. Twitter as well as Facebook have a broad appeal and, consequently, can be utilized by freelancers working in all areas. Other social media platforms that are popular are: YouTube, LinkedIn, Pinterest, Tumblr, SnapChat and Google+.

Facebook

Facebook is the biggest percentage of social media's users. With 1.97 billion users active, Facebook is the first platform you can utilize to create your presence on social media. Create an account on Facebook and asking your Facebook contacts to join it. This will be your initial fan base.

The most important thing to add to your Facebook profile is the video. I fell in love Facebook Live. Facebook Live feature and used it to create an introductory video that I uploaded to my Facebook page. Facebook Live is an awesome method to interact with your audience. You can allow them to comment on, share and like your live stream while you're recording. You can respond to comments and questions and engage your fans effectively. The more engaging the content is and the more people will be inclined to share the video. This leads to a growing number of fan base.

The most important thing for Facebook Live videos is attracting viewers. Plan a time and date to upload your video, and then promote it to friends on Facebook as well as your family. Make sure it's scheduled at an hour when more users are likely to be on Facebook. Hootsuite basing their experiences, recommends posting on Wednesday, Monday, and Friday from 12pm to 3pm, and on Saturdays and Sundays between 1pm and 12pm as the most effective times to publish Facebook postings. Try the times you post and determine which ones work best for your followers.

Facebook Pages are a myriad options to interact with your followers. They can organize events and promotions and then share images or videos as well as articles. Utilize your CMS to distribute as many posts as you can. Display any promotions or specials and invite your fans to connect with you.

The Facebook's PPC advertising option allows you to gain more exposure for your Facebook webpage and Facebook page. Create an account on Facebook Ads Account and utilize an Account Manager to create your Ads Account Manager to design the first advertising. These tips can help in creating an effective Facebook advertisement that is seen.

Keywords

In the majority of chapters in this book since they're crucial. Your ads won't be seen by people in the absence of correct words. Additionally, the price per click of an advertisement will be affected by the keyword you select. PPC advertising is in essence the equivalent of a bidding battle in which you compete to get your advert ranked with your chosen keywords. Make use of Google Adword's Keyword Planner tool to help you choose the appropriate terms for your ads.

Audience

It will prompt you to select type of gender, the location and age group, as well as interests of the audience you are targeting. Be aware of the type of people you wish to connect with. What are their locations? What is their age? What kind of activities do they do? The right target audience can make it much more likely that those are going to click on your ads. The more views your advertisement is able to get, the better its relevance score. Higher scores on relevancy increase the CPC of your ad and consequently, guarantees that your advertisement is seen by more potential customers.

A/B Testing

Effective marketers will test an ad against an alternative. It is possible to make minor or significant changes in order to determine what appeals to your target audience. The goal is to analyze every ad's performance when they're running and find out the reasons which make one advertisement more successful than others.

Content

Your target audience may be right on. If your material does not have the appropriate appeal, the results won't come through. The right images and words are vital. Provide deals and offers which will entice everyone who views the advertisement. You might consider using explainer videos or animated videos. Make every effort to make your material more appealing.

Twitter

Facebook has the biggest online audience for social media. But, PPC advertising on Facebook could be very costly. Twitter is a great alternative to Facebook to help people locate your posts easily using Hash tags. It's not even necessary to set up an Twitter Business accounts. The hashtags and mentions will do all the work.

Twitter has around 317 million active users. Hash tags help users to discover content relevant to the topics they are concerned about. When you utilize hash tags that are related to posts you publish on Twitter People will discover them. Create content that is interesting that they'll join your account.

Additionally, Twitter provides the perfect method to test your advertising creativity. Anything you wish to convey can be written within just 140 words or less. Develop your lines and you will bring people to talk about your business.

Then, Twitter has two more functions that I find fascinating: polls as well as a live streaming. The polls allow you to get comments from your users on the topics you select. People can vote in realtime. It's an excellent option to gather instant feedback on your business. The live stream on Twitter is operated by Periscope which functions in the same way as facebook's live stream. But, users can only make comments during the live stream but not later.

Chapter 7: The Decision Making Process
Go Freelance

I've spoken to many e-Learning designers that are thinking about going freelance and I'm able to see the spark of my passion in them, a desire to be creative as well as a desire to become more in charge of their career. The idea of going freelance, for a lot it is easy to view as a way to alleviate the strain and restrictions of a professional work-from-home job. What can be more satisfying than having being able to choose which projects to work at and what time?

When I started my journey as an online e-Learning designer on a contract basis I was extremely excited at the possibilities that my future success would be entirely in my hands! I could finally have the opportunity be able to devote my time imaginative! I've always dreamed of having the opportunity to get away from the responsibilities of my job and pursue my passion to create top-quality e-learning tools for my customers.

Then, realisation hit: I owned running my own company, and I had to deal with a lot of overhead that took up a large portion the time. It was my personal marketing department. and my personal accounting team. My own legal team. Before I had even started my first course I had many hours of work which was not at all connected to my passion for online learning.

I'm happy with the decision to work as a freelancer regardless of the economic aspect that comes with it, I've experienced plenty in terms of satisfaction at work, and I've gained a lot of knowledge during the course of my journey. Before we dive deep into the details of how you can start an e-learning business that is freelance I'd like to talk about what you're engaging in before you take the leap!

The Pros and Cons of e-Learning Freelancing

There is no perfect situation therefore, you need to take into consideration both benefits and drawbacks of being a freelancer as opposed to employed full-time for the same company. As I mentioned that I enjoy being working as a freelancer. However, it is important to bear your mind open to the possibility that you will differ. What sounds as an "pro" to me may be interpreted as an "con" to you.

The best aspect of working as freelance is the versatility and control that it gives. This is what I like about it:

The time you spend is yours. I enjoy controlling my time. I'm not the type of person who gets up in the morning which is why being able get my day started anytime I'd like is an absolute pleasure.

There is no politics in the office. Being a freelancer, I do not have to be concerned about the games that frequently happens in offices. It is completely safe to avoid issues such as the rumor mill, the constant reorganization of responsibilities and roles, and fretting about who's telling me what to say about myself. It's a huge delight!

You decide the people you collaborate with. I've found that certain customers or projects don't seem to be a good suit for me. whenever I suspect a lack of match, I've got the option of leaving.

Don't rely on other people to succeed. I've had many excellent coworkers in the past However, when it comes the matter of it all, I like to be the sole person who is accountable for my actions. Even though it creates a lot of stress for me, I'm happy with it for the basic reason that I do not have to fret about any other person's work (or absence of). When I freelance there are times when I have subcontract work on larger assignments (for instance, for Voice-over Artists as well as other e-Learning Designers) And in these situations, I'm sure I scrutinize any work that I get from a subcontractor.

You can participate in various tasks. I've worked as an E-Learning Designer in the famous widget factory and will tell you that After a while it becomes boring to work with widgets. Being a freelancer, I work with clients in a variety of fields and across different nations which creates diverse work environment which helps me avoid exhaustion.

A freelance life has disadvantages. Let's take a examine some motives to consider to work in an e-Learning full-time job with a reputable firm.

Benefits. Health insurance benefits and retirement plans and vacation pay are huge. Health care costs is astronomical on a per-individual basis. And as freelancers, if I choose to travel and I'm not paid. If you're thinking of becoming an independent contractor, ensure you've got a plan in place for such things!

Steady Income. When you work as a freelancer, it's not uncommon for work to be irregular. During certain times I'll be working far more than I'm able to handle or manage, while other months I'll have to endure a drought. It's fine for me however, it's crucial to be aware that a regular income from a company can give tranquility.

A Defined Career Path. The best business will offer a specific career path that is laid out in front of you. And continued growth will bring raises as well as change of titles. Being a freelancer my only options to gain a promotion is by getting additional clients (which implies working longer hours) as well as making my current clients pay higher costs (which might cause them to feel angry). If you think the "corporate ladder" is valuable for you, then you might consider rethinking becoming a freelancer.

Administrative Overhead. Like I said at the start of this chapter the sole proprietor of my business comes with lots of expenses.

Being a freelancer, I devote a significant amount of time in marketing myself, keeping track of my expenses as well as managing my personal website. Together, they consume a lot of money and time! Prior to stepping into the freelance market, take into consideration that, while you'll be the chief executive officer of your business, you'll also be the person who cleans up (not to say there's nothing to be concerned about).

Co-workers. Though I often get angry with office politics but I sometimes do wish I had coworkers with whom who I could bounce ideas off and to socialize with. Being a freelancer can be lonely and it's essential to be ready for isolation, even if you like solitude. It's also important to make plans for socializing with coworkers.

The lists above were based on my individual preferences. Yours may differ from mine, and that's fine. While you're deciding for yourself, be sure to take the idea of working from home as a whole-heartedly--any job is a work however, no job can be ideal!

Freelance Life: Destination, or Refuge?

One reason I believe it's crucial to think about whether or not you should go freelance is the fact that I've observed several people make the decision independently based upon doubtful motives. My experience has shown that the majority of people who say "I'm considering going freelance," the majority of them are really saying is "I'm unhappy in my current job and I need a change."

Many people approach this from a different perspective However, as I pointed out in the beginning of this article it's simple to become exuberant about the benefits of a working from home without taking into account all of reality. It was my experience that I did the same thing to a certain extent. Freelancing is the ideal option for me due to various reasons. However, sincere, "getting away from a day job that was a bad fit" was definitely at the top of my checklist! Thinking of the freelance life as the"greener" grass is completely normal. However, when you're preparing to transition I would suggest that you consider whether you're trying to find a new job instead of trying to escape the job I'm currently working at?

The truth is that there's no correct or incorrect answer to this issue. You could become a successful freelancer in e-Learning whatever your motive. However, it's crucial to understand the motivation behind your decision to work on your own as you might have to be able to handle your own expectations. If you're hoping for your freelance lifestyle to be a life that allows you to create all of the time, and never having to face the stress of work again it's likely that you'll be disappointed by the reality. If you approach it with a clear understanding of the reason you're doing this and why you're doing it, you're better off being successful.

Testing the Waters

It's important to note that moving from working a full-time job to freelance isn't an instant, dramatic shift. Some freelancers start with "testing the waters" while they're employed by a well-established firm, for instance, through a variety of projects at night and during weekends. "Part-time freelancing" can be the ideal way to experience an idea of life without the risk of moving to a freelancing way of life.

"Part-time freelancing" can be useful, but it's usually difficult to sustain. You can certainly work at two jobs. But I've found that while earning money can be nice it's not worth sacrificing your evenings or weekends wasn't always worthwhile. Additionally, freelancers who work part-time are often left out of lucrative projects and contracts. It's difficult to compete for new big-scale projects when you're dedicated to full-time work on behalf of another person. Additionally, most companies have "no moonlighting" clauses in the terms of their contracts for employees, so prior to deciding on the next job aside from your regular job be sure that you're adhering to any agreements that you've entered into!

After you've outlined the reasons you're interested in becoming an e-Learning designer on a contract basis, you're now ready to answer the second big issue: what exactly do you expect to do when you take on this new job?

Chapter 8: Knowing Your Goals

Before taking the plunge into becoming an e-Learning freelancer consider: What do I want to accomplish?

Although it may seem to be something that isn't important however, you may be amazed by the amount of people who do not follow this advice which means they waste time beginning a career as a freelancer without a way of measuring the success of their work. It was me, too at the time I started my freelance career as I was aware of the freedom and flexibility in a free-lance career However, I wasn't defining the goals I wanted to achieve for my first year. I spent my time doing tasks that I could complete and never thought about the kind of work I was supposed to do. I was aware that I would like to find jobs that could help me advance in my career However, I didn't stop to think about the type of job that could be required to achieve the job.

You should think about the goals you'd like to accomplish in the coming year. While you're considering your professional objectives as a freelancer take a look at some of the typical goals that new freelancers face.

Goals That Can Lead to Burnout

In many instances, when I question colleagues what they are hoping to accomplish in their freelance careers, they'll mention exactly the same two elements:

1. Earning money. It's simple to glance at the hourly rate of freelancers and say "I would definitely make so much more money if I went solo!" However, before you put the down payment for that new Ferrari be aware the fact that working as self-employed comes with significant expenses, including the monthly Internet expenses to the new estimates for quarterly taxes. You can certainly earn an adequate income working being a freelance designer of e-

Learning However, it's going require time. Remember that a majority of small companies do not turn into a profit within their first year.

2. Being in control of your working hours and time. Being a freelancer You'll have complete charge of the amount and what you work. Be aware that you're likely to find that at the beginning, you'll have to work longer hours than in a normal full-time job. If, for instance, you're planning to freelance part-time in order to be able to be more at home with your loved ones, you should consider it that initially it could mean you're working longer than you would at a full-time job to get the best clients or projects to take on.

If you're an Learning & Development professional, it is likely that your intuitions are kickin' into high gear and telling you "But this isn't a goal but outcomes! The real goal has tangible effects." It's true that you'd be right, however being e-Learning experts it's easy to overlook the basic principles of a well-planned goal setting. When you are beginning writing your goals, be aware that you'll require to be clearer than just saying you're looking to earn profits and manage your schedule!

Prior to writing my personal goals, I believed that I was in the hands of whatever jobs were available. It wasn't until I started creating out my personal goals that I began to believe that I had control over my destiny (which was among the motivations to go freelance initially).

Getting Started Writing Your Own Goals

What's the most effective method of defining your personal objectives? The most important action is to put your goals down. Be aware that easy and simple do not mean the same! There's a wealth of info available on setting goals (you are probably acquainted with "S.M.A.R.T. goals" that could be helpful for this task) It's well beneficial to select the technique is most suitable for your needs. However, the most important thing is this exercise, and remember that until you write your goals down, they're not real.

Write down your goals and objectives gives an opportunity to look at your own goals. Have you established a goal which defines what work is going to make you happy? When will you be able to tell if you've achieved your goal? Is your goal a reflection of your ideal work-life balance that you hope to attain?

One of my professional goals is to aid others who are e-Learning Designers, through sharing my experiences through my own experience as a freelancer. When I first wrote this goal down I was able to create my own criteria for success and what steps I'd take in order to reach it (for example, in this book).

While you write your goal keep these suggestions in mind:

Note down separate short-term, long-term and ongoing objectives. If you're just beginning there's a good chance you'll have plans for finding work and organizing your life. Be sure to note the things you would like the future of your career to look like and how you'd like your daily practices to implement.

Don't think just about your strengths, but make sure that you've identified the job you're passionate about. If, for instance, you are a fan of creating tests, create a plan on the subject.

Write down goals to help you keep your skills up to date. Being up to date with the latest techniques for e-learning is crucial So don't forget to write goals that are addressing continuing training needs!

Write down continuous targets that are geared towards the type of life you would like to live. In other words, when you plan the time you'll need to dedicate to your career goals, make sure you make time to take proper care of your own needs. Fitness is something that could easily be neglected when at my wits end, and so I've devoted my weekly workout time for my ongoing goals.

Be sure to review your goals regularly as well as to make new goals when you've accomplished the old ones.

Quantify as many as you're able. If you're looking for a lot of customers, indicate the number you'd like to have. If you're looking to expand the number of followers you have on Twitter, indicate the number of followers you're looking for.

Be sure to share your goals with your colleagues for their feedback. An additional opinion could be very beneficial!

Share your objectives on social media. This will allow others to be supportive of you.

Additionally, you'll also have taken that extra step of making a commitment to your objectives more openly.

Good Goals vs. Bad Goals

It is my suggestion that you examine your goals' quality in order to ensure that you're preparing yourself to be successful. There's plenty of information regarding the essential elements that make up a successful goals (again I suggest the S.M.A.R.T. framework is extremely helpful in this regard) However, it may occasionally be difficult to recognize an unsuitable goal, one that's not stated in a way to help you get there.

The most commonly used "bad goals" that I observe share some characteristics:

Objectives that are too general. If there is any metrics that are associated with the target, it's impossible to determine if it's been achieved or not. There are a number of goals which begin with "To raise awareness about ...", which is usually an indicator to me that the person who wrote it isn't prepared be a part of achieving something (unless they're monitoring the level of awareness they have, which is rare).

Impossible goals. Do not use your goals for your "vision board." It's crucial to ensure that the goals you establish for yourself fall within your reach, and do not go beyond the limits of reality.

It's important to set goals that won't be a challenge for anybody. Although it's tempting to make easy-to-get-to fruit but it's crucial to be sure you're setting the right goals.

Sample Goals

To provide an illustration, I've included the following goals as examples. Initially I wasn't sure if it was appropriate to share examples since I'm trying to stop those from stealing someone else's goal-setting strategies. Your goals must reflect your own personal goals of the goals you'd like to accomplish in your own way, rather than a standardized checklist! However, I recognize how challenging it may be to start with goal-setting, which is why I've included a handful of my resolutions for 2017 to give you an idea of the range of the topics, details, and areas the goals will be covering. When you're reviewing them think about what your personal goals could be.

2017 Goals

Short-Term (Next 12 months)

Create a new site using an StudioPress template prior to January 10, 2017.

3. Create and publish three (3) E-books that are based upon the e-Learning Business Series by October 15th 17th, 2017.

Write 2 (2) blogs as guest entries for the e-Learning Heroes blog until December 1, 2017.

Long-Term (> 12 months)

Create at least 2 streams of passive income that produce at least $XX,XXX each calendar year as of December 1st, 2018.

o Repay your home mortgage on or before April 1st, 2026.

Continuous (Ongoing)

Review/update the accounts record (expenses revenues, expenses (cash flow, expenses, invoicing) every Friday

o Recognize and acknowledge at least one individual that has helped me in my personal/professional endeavors by the last Friday of each month.

Keep in mind that the following are my goals for both professional and personal. Your goals you set for yourself must be those that actually are important and that resonate with your personal values. Doing the same thing as others can make you want to imitate the way they do. Set your goals as the basis for determining the things that make you different! This is the same for income goals, and also defining the definition of what "success" looks like.

When you've set your goals then you're placed in a more powerful situation. While you look at the available jobs and your options, you will be able to hold yourself accountable. Will this job bring you one step closer to one of your objectives? Are you given an opportunity to develop by the means you would like to? If you define what success means, you've made your own compass which is, hopefully can lead you to personal happiness.

Chapter 9: Why It's Important To Know Your Core Goals And Values

If you have your professional objectives established, it's now time to focus on something as vital: your primary beliefs as an e-Learning designer.

The goals you've set out will assist you in deciding the goals you'd like to achieve as an e-Learning designer, the values you hold dear can help determine what you'll do to achieve this. Writing your values down in the form of a document is your opportunity to expressly define how you'd like to operate, both with others and yourself.

What Core Values Are, and Aren't

Your core values comprise short statements which describe the way you'd like to apply in your job, as well as what you'll strive to achieve in your professional life. Imagine the core values you hold as your individual personal professional GPS that is continuously guiding you to your goals and the processes that leave you feeling the most satisfied. Although our objectives can keep us motivated and help us to gauge the progress we make, our fundamental values can be quite different. The core values you choose to follow are your individual code of conduct and clearly defined values will help to ensure you're following this code of conduct.

When you are a freelancer, your fundamental values are particularly important because they will assist you in choosing the projects and clients that you would like to take on, and also what you can and should not do.

Here is an example of one of my principles:

Simplicity. My business philosophy is to keep things easy and understandable for my customers. My goal is to eliminate the clutter that is a part of my processes and products to ensure that only what is necessary and essential elements remain.

After a lot of thought, I realized that the simplicity of my approach was among my most important values since I could apply it to how I interact with my clients and also the documents I write for my clients. As an example, whenever I start an business relationship with the first client I will always draft the Statement of Work (the document which outlines what I'm planning to accomplish for them). When I write each Statement of Work, I check it against my fundamental values of simplicity. Is the document simple and easy to read? Did I include any irrelevant data that I'm able to cut out? In the same way, when creating online learning content to be used by them, this fundamental importance is used for a basis test to determine if I've presented the information learners need to be aware of as easily as is possible? Do I have any information that doesn't need to be included?

It's crucial that my values aren't just a chant but serve a useful reason that allows me to be sure that I'm adhering to my professional expectations I've established for myself. It's crucial: the values you set for yourself need be practical ideas are applicable to everyday making decisions. If you're able use your values to this extent--use to establish a point of reference for yourself--you've created solid value-based core values. If you're able to identify yourself as a fan of some idea, but you aren't able to find a feasible way to apply it, this could be an indication that you have to make the idea an actual core value.

It's important to remember the fact that values of core are distinct from the mission statement or slogan. There are many businesses that publish"values" or "values," but in the real world, they're using words that are good to market their products. Think about some classic assertions that are popular, such as "quality is job one," or "the customer is always right." Both concepts sound fantastic, however it's a difficult task to implement them every day. They are intentions, which are great, but they aren't an actual behavior that you can achieve the standard they are.

How to Define Your Own Core Values

How do you find your own fundamental beliefs? It's not easy but it's worthwhile taking the time. When you're deciding on your own personal values, ensure that you have plenty of time to think about yourself and the things that are important to you as well as your work. The core values you choose to follow must be a reflection of your personal insights about what you value, who you are and what is most important for you.

While I was writing down my personal values, I made a commitment to an hour every day, for the duration of the duration of a week. There is a chance that you'll need greater or lesser time. that's the only duration that has worked for me. In that period I was thinking about the some of my work-related experiences and the things that made me feel positive or negative over those particular events. I began jotting notes about what worked for me, and what did not work for my personal needs. It was then that I began to search at the patterns I came up with, patterns that revealed commonality in every aspect that worked for my personal needs. (One pattern that came to mind to me was that those events that I did not want to repeat, were all messy and complicated, which led me to think about including "simplicity" as one of my primary principles.)

When I'd discovered a few themes which were positive as well as negative, I decided to take some time to think about their significance. This was not easy as I was needing to focus the themes I was focusing on and figure out the ones that would take me towards the direction I would like to go in both as a person and professional. The importance of simplicity was at the top of my checklist, and once I had that I was able to create drafts that reflected this core quality. In the end, I pushed myself to to think about this and provide myself with the benefits of careful examination. When I was thinking about my desire to be simple I looked at how this could apply to my relationships with clients and my work I made sure the draft version of this fundamental value addressed both.

After I finished with my six values that I was able to identify, and I printed them off and hung them up in my office for me to remember to utilize them. It is possible to have more than six or even less, but I've found that most people can benefit from between 5 and 8 key values (if you're more than that then you might find it challenging to keep using these). When your core values are set, be sure that they're in a location where you can view them and use them quickly. My values are posted at my desk while reviewing them at early in the morning is a great way to encourage me to begin my work.

Take a look on online for others' fundamental values to get ideas for your own. There are a few good ones in the world! However, be aware that following someone else's principles might not be a way to achieve the success you desire. The process of establishing your own core values is an individual process, although it's great to learn from the principles others have written about however, you must be sure that the values you choose to follow reflect your own values by focusing on your own personal values. Be aware that there's an abundance of non-practical and generic values that are out there So, you must scrutinize each and think about what you could use it in the tasks you create as well as the relationships with clients you manage.

What Happens if You Don't Write Core Values?

It takes some time to develop and define It is a challenge to define them, and I know the ease of being able to put off work or get distracted by another task that is more urgent. However, the earlier you identify your fundamental values and then write your values down, the faster you'll achieve your personal level of success by ensuring that you're living the standards you have set yourself.

If you don't write down your the core values of your organization, you are taking various risks. Keep in mind the saying that says: "If you don't stand for something, you'll fall for anything!" Prior to the time I was able to articulate my primary values as an eLearning Designer, I encountered various difficult situations My decisions were not consistent and my processes were hampered due to the my concessions as well as, most importantly I let others who were around me decide my values. Consider the GPS concept: it's very easy to get lost in the shuffle with no the foundational values I had I didn't know whether I would ever get to my optimal professional status.

Walk the Walk

When you've completed the core values you want to live by and have written the values down, ensure they are easily accessible. If you keep your core values close it's much easier to utilize the values as a resource instead of a workout.

Even though you shouldn't worry about them too much but it is important to create a timing or schedule for how you monitor your goals. As of the time, I've added the value check-in into my regular routines. That ensures that I'm not just asking the appropriate questions, but also asking them at just the right moment. In the example above, prior to I begin the proposal for a project I review my values to ensure that I'm doing the right thing.

One of my main values revolves around the notion of honesty. In the course of examining my core values frequently When I'm preparing to present a proposal to a potential client I will often go through it to ensure I'm not offering them options or services that they do not require. Some freelancers have padded their proposal with irrelevant material or even activities that I do not personally think it's good. If you're dealing with a customer that isn't educated enough to be aware the fact that they're not getting any value from the services they're paying for and you're getting a kick out of the client! Integrity is a top priority for me and it's an excellent way of making sure I'm "walking the walk."

Alongside assessing how your work is in line with your values, it's essential to apply these values to consider the way your recent choices and behavior coincide with the core values. It's not a self-guided assessment of performance, but rather this is your opportunity to consider, "Did I live up to the ideal my core values on this e-Learning project?" If you believe you did not, it may be beneficial to know the reasons behind it, and then decide to make a different choice in the future.

I've always been amazed by how fast implementing goals have brought about positive changes for me in my freelancing life. One example of my priorities is the work-life harmony.

Work-Life Balance. My business strategy is to ensure a clear line between my work as well as my personal life. I'll focus my attention at each one separately.

This value was written after I realized that I struggled to separate from my work-from-home life. I didn't want to lose out on the chance as I would like my customers to know that I was accessible. However, by having to be "always on" for my clients, I wasn't afforded plenty of time to unwind and was often being forced to tell my family members to be patient when I was working all day long. As I pondered it I came to realize that this wasn't the way I intended to lead my life.

With the idea of balancing work and life at that point, I became more confident to stick in line with it and create solutions so my clients don't be left feeling cheated. I began putting aside times in my calendar to spend with my family, and also using techniques for managing my time (like that of the Pomodoro Technique). After I had put my beliefs in practice, my freelancing life was a more suitable fit for me.

Chapter 10: The Essential Tools For Launching Your Business

In the beginning of your career as a freelancer in e-Learning is likely that your budget for the equipment and tools is likely to be limited. A few expenses, including the purchase of a computer or Internet connectivity, will to be crucial to get your company up and running, whereas others are best left until you've completed the initial projects and are earning money. In this article I'll share my tips on the equipment, software as well as services you'll require when you embark on your freelance e-learning career.

Before we begin some quick cautions regarding the services and products I'll cover throughout this section:

Technology changes constantly and it's quite possible that my hardware may be obsolete at the time that you read this. That's OK! It is best to view each advice as a kind of classification instead of a particular product. So, for instance, if I recommend the Samsung Galaxy as my smartphone and you're not required be rushing to exchange your iPhone. What's important is that your smartphone is a vital element of your freelance existence.

I do not have any affiliation to any of the names or brands listed on this page.

Hardware and Office Equipment

The first of most significant investments you'll make is in the computer you have. Choosing the correct machine for you is a major decision since it will be the primary tool you use for at the very least several years. Choosing to skimp on essential features may result in you spending both time and money in the longer term.

This is also an excellent opportunity to consider that the vast majority equipment you purchase for freelance work is tax deductible and can therefore assist in decreasing the amount you must pay to the federal government. Although that doesn't mean that you have to invest a lot of money in the latest equipment, it does suggest that you've the ability to spend more as a business owner of a small size that you do as an average consumer. (In Chapter 7, I'll talk about the different kinds of professionals to help you control your costs, deductions and tax obligations.)

How powerful is your system have to be? If you think about it, when you create online courseware it will be necessary to build edit, publish, and modify massive, high-quality documents, and this can be processing- and memory-intensive. The majority of other things that you'll need to perform, such as email as well as web-based meeting, etc.-- will not require a significant amount of work. Below are the specifications for my computer's desktop:

Windows 10 Pro (64-bit edition)

Intel chip, i7 4790 CPU @ 3.60 GHz

16GB of RAM

*120GB SSD Hard Drive (main OS drive)

Western Digital 4TB external SATA hard drive (for local data storage)

Western Digital 4TB MyBook USB hard drive (for system back-ups)

NVIDIA GeForce GTX 750ti 2GB video card

27" monitor

I designed this machine to support my career as a freelance instructor with in my mind. It has a top-of-the-line processor, lots of RAM, a solid state hard drive and superior video card. I made an investment in hardware to accelerate my production. And even though a less powerful computer might definitely suffice however, I wanted to be sure my investment could be able to last for at least 3 years. (Also I'm an avid Windows person, however purchasing an Mac could be a good alternative, as long as it comes with the same specs.)

Laptops and desktops. Desktops in e-Learning

Although I would prefer the desktop as my primary computer however, a lot of my freelance coworkers like laptops because of their mobility. There's not a "right" answer when it is determining which model of computer will work most suitable for the creation of e-Learning material and it comes down to your own personal preferences.

If you're trying to decide, the two most important questions you should be asking yourself are:

How often should I anticipate that I will require a trip using my laptop?

Do I have the money to buy an laptop with enough power?

Mobility at first appears to be an important aspect to freelance work, however I would encourage you to think about your needs in a critical manner and objectively. It's inevitable that you'll be in contact with your clients at times, so having a PC available during these sessions could prove crucial. In my experience using a laptop during meetings is often distracting as well. Nine times out of 10 times, when I've had a laptop in the presence of clients, it was to record notes. After I started attending meetings carrying the legal pad, tablet, and a pen (just to be prepared) I noticed that meetings to be just as productive and that I didn't need to carry around an entire bag of laptop with its various accessories. Also, your circumstances and needs will be different However, prior to shelling out the money to buy a new laptop, consider whether I really require my computer along with me everywhere?

Additionally, you should spend your time pondering the cost-to-speed ratio when using laptops. In the example of specifications that I have described earlier for my laptop If I was to purchase a laptop with the same specs that I could end up having to pay about double. It's not at a bargain! The higher cost of laptops can be an acceptable expense, since you're paying for the capability to be able to work wherever you want, as that you don't make any sacrifices to performance. If you're considering purchasing a laptop with a lower price tag because it's more affordable Be aware that each decision you make could result in your online learning production getting slower as you could be disappointed in buying the wrong machine.

Testing Devices

Although a smartphone is important to keep your company running however, you must be aware that it has serve as more than the phone itself, but to test all the content that you create for customers. For me I'm using an Samsung Galaxy, because I would like a smartphone that can help to ensure that my content is designed to work with a standard

Android phone. To test my content on Apple devices, I use a 4th-generation iPad.

Office Basics

You should have some basic skills for communication! The following are the things I would recommend learning:

Copier/Scanner/Fax/Printer. My goal is to often eliminate paper, however there are occasions that nothing is better than the physical copies of an item. The scanner that is built-in to my computer can be a great help the times when I have to convert drawings I've made into a computer in situations where I must make a signature, scan or send documents back to clients.

Landline Phone or Cell Phone. Although the majority of people would prefer just a mobile phone but a landline can be an acceptable choice too. The most essential thing is to are able to have a telephone and number devoted for your business. It's not just that having a separate phone number help in the tracking of your company's phone costs significantly easier, it'll also keep you from having customers make calls to your personal line during the wrong time!

Wireless Headset. Be aware that you'll require both hands on the table during most conversations with your clients. You'll want to keep notes and noting down ideas. In addition, long calls aren't easy using handheld phones. Although not everybody will think this is necessary, it's vital for me be able to roam around free of tethers and that's why I have the OfficeRunner Wireless Headset Essential Bundle of Sennheiser.

Software

The first thing you're likely to face when you're establishing up your company is that the cost of software can add up! It is important to put the funds you budgeted for the cost of software, specifically in the case of annual upgrades which are usually worthy of spending money for. Though a large portion of the applications I've recommended will require purchase however, there are many excellent software programs that are free and can be an integral part of your toolset. Since I'm a freelancer and looking to reduce costs I'm constantly on the search for open source software. I'm aware that I'll have to buy the majority of my essential software applications.

Software for Developing Learning Materials Microsoft Office (Outlook; Word; PowerPoint; Excel). While I know it's hipper to use Google Docs these days, the reality is that many businesses--especially large corporate businesses, who can be very loyal, lucrative clients--are still using the Office suite of applications. Although you may be more at ease with a different office suite but it's important for many different client environments that you are able to utilize the format of files you're comfortable working with.

Camtasia Studio. Camtasia is my preferred video editor because I've found it to provide the perfect blend of sophisticated and user-friendliness. I don't require a fully-featured software for video production like Adobe Premiere, but I really need a software which can assist me in creating short, quality videos as Camtasia Studio helps me do it. Camtasia can also be used to create basic, low-cost educational content. It can be a good option for those who don't require the entire feature set offered by Articulate Storyline or Articulate 360.

Articulate Storyline and/or Articulate 360. It's probably the largest investment in software that you can make for your e-Learning company. You'll require a recent version of Storyline from Articulate for all of your e-Learning production needs. Their daily community challenges provide the perfect opportunity to study the latest techniques from fellow designers as well as network with other designers of e-Learning.

In the past, I've updated to Articulate 360 that comprises Storyline 360, Studio 360, Replay 360, Peek Preso Content, Library, Articulate Review, Articulate Live, and Rise.

SnagIt. You'll need an efficient and simple screen capture and marking-up tool. I've used SnagIt for several years and their interface for users is really evolving. All major operating systems include integrated screen capture tools built in There are a lot of third-party options for free, such as Jing, Skitch, or FastStone Capture.

Audacity. I utilize Audacity (a open source, free software) to perform the majority of my recording as well as editing. This helps me ensure that my audio recordings are as clear and as clean as they have to be. (Also I should point out that you can also use Camtasia Studio for audio recordings too.)

Xmind. It is a great mind-map tool allows me to think through and plan my ideas for any assignment.

Adobe Kuler. Kuler is a program that allows you to design colors that aids in designing the appearance and feel of educational materials.

Adobe Photoshop Creative Cloud and Lightroom Creative Cloud. Sometimes, I use photos that I've created for my own content using the programs to alter my photographs. Even though Adobe subscriptions cost a bit, Photoshop and Lightroom are worth the cost (you have the option of a subscription to Adobe Photoshop as well as Adobe Lightroom at around $9.99 each month).

Pixie. The ability to match colors is important. Pixie allows you to point at an color and will give you the RGB HTML, CMYK, and HSV value for the color.

To interact with customers:

DropBox. All of the file sharing for my clients with DropBox because the vast majority of my clients are registered with DropBox accounts. (Google Drive, Amazon Drive, and Box.com are all popular alternatives to DropBox to store and share files as well as being perfectly acceptable options.)

WebEx. WebEx remains the standard in desktop sharing and web-based conferencing for good reason. When you sign up for the free account, you can host conference calls as little as two participants and one host. (For my clients that prefer Skype I use the Skype application.)

Articulate TempShare. The Articulate TempShare program (which is available for free) permits me to temporarily upload Storyline contents and also generate an unguessable URL to share my work to others. It is extremely useful for looking over drafts and is compatible in conjunction with Articulate Storyline.

TweetDeck. Twitter is essential for networking and interacting with people working in the field of e-Learning, however, it is also a resource to potential customers. TweetDeck assists me in treating my Twitter profile as a part of my storefronts for my business.

Your website's URL:

My website runs WordPress and I host everything through BlueHost.

To make my website appear professional, I am using StudioPress to create WordPress themes as well as plugins.

I use also an WordPress plugin named "Embed Articulate to WordPress" via eLearningfreak.com. This plugin allows me to post the content of Articulate Storyline as well as Articulate 360 directly to my website.

Contact form for my website was designed with Gravity Forms. Along with the questions I pose in the SurveyMonkey forms, allows me to record and keep track of my questions from potential customers.

I am using MailChimp for managing my month-long Newsletter.

Digital Assets

If you're developing learning content You'll require an arsenal of resources, including buttons, stock photography or icons. It's easy to be lost if you do not know where to find them. Below are some of the sources I typically get my digital assets

E-Learningart.com has templates that are specifically designed for the Articulate Storyline platform, as well as images for materials designed for online learning although their collections don't have the same size as rival e-Learning Brothers, they are cheaper.

123rf.com is another service which offers thousands of royalty-free images. I usually use this website in the event that I cannot find the appropriate photos elsewhere However, it is not recommended to use them in excess, since they depend on a credit system which makes it simple to pay a large amount of cash.

*The Articulate e-Learning Heroes Community, that I previously mentioned includes its own library of graphics, buttons pictures, icons and buttons.

FreeSFX offers an extensive collection of audio files for study resources. Everything they have is completely absolutely free. However, they require that you acknowledge them when you utilize their products.

Chapter 11: Setting Up Your Business

If you're the first E-Learning freelancer, you'll have to make several major choices you'll have to make concerning the legality of setting up your business. A few of these options could have significant implications in the amount you pay taxed and the risk that you're personally choosing to take, making it essential to make sure you're well aware, and thoughtful in each and every decision. In this section I'll discuss what I consider to be the most significant choices as well as highlighting areas that which you should research prior to making a decision.

Before we get started before we begin, let me clarify that This is not an attorney or financial advisor or accountant, and the advice I'll provide isn't a substitute for advice from a lawyer or accountant. You should not take action on any of the information below information without conducting research independently or consulting with a professional. The laws and the best practices may differ in each state and sometimes the city and state. This article's goal is to help you think about what kind of questions that you'll need to address. In the event of kicking an old horse, there is nothing better than the guidance of an expert you trust.

The decision-making process of deciding how you structure your company could be overwhelming and, frankly, dull But when you take the time to make good decision for you You'll save yourself many hours later on and will avoid possible risks that can have devastating negative consequences. Like I said at the beginning of the book I'm trying to assist you in navigating the maze of paperwork and complexities to allow you to be able to focus on what you do best!

There are three areas to think about when it comes in establishing a freelance enterprise:

1. The separation of your personal and business financials;

2. Selection of the correct legally-conforming business structure

3. The most efficient ways to pay taxes.

1. Transactions: You've Got to Keep 'Em Separated

The first and most important thing is that it is essential to ensure that you've separated the business transactions from private ones. Though this may seem obvious but keeping track of your finances separately can be a very easy thing to overlook in the event that you do not manage to follow this procedure and you don't, you'll end up with a host of problems when it comes to the IRS. This is especially true in the event of being investigated. Furthermore, based on the structure of your business that you decide to use (more about this later) There could exist a legal obligation for them to be separated.

Solving Separation Anxiety: Finding a Bank You Trust

The first step towards making sure your company's finances are independent is to establish an account for your business with the bank you choose to use. Be careful, as the way the bank runs has an effect on the day-to-day activities. While deciding on the bank I was thinking about the following aspects:

Location and customer service. I want to be aware that, if I have a question that I have the option of speaking to an individual bank representative regarding it, rather than wait on the telephone waiting for a customer service department to assist me.

The availability of electronic deposits and wire transfer. Most of my customers pay me with checks, which is why I chose to look for the bank that offered the option of free electronic deposit. Furthermore, I work with international customers, which is why accepting wire transfer payments was crucial to my needs.

Paper checking. It's my goal to be as paper-free as I can. But in my company, I'm more secure with an audit trail that tracks each transaction. I ensured that the financial institution I chose could allow this.

It's possible that you have specific preferences for the bank that you pick, so spend the time to create an outline of what you'll require, then look into which institutions can (or are unable to) fulfill your requirements. Be sure to contact the bank and ask questions! Making a call prior to the time is essential since the institution which you select may need the submission of specific documents required for a small business account. You'll need to be aware of these requirements prior to the deadline.

If you've decided on a banking institution you want to visit, do so in person and try to develop a connection with an agent. Although you might not have the opportunity to speak to the exact person at all times however, it's always a good idea to get in touch with the bank's representative that can assist you in your choices. Consider the fact that your company's needs could alter over time as your business develops. It can be useful to speak with an individual at the bank that is familiar with your business's needs from the very beginning.

2. Architecting Your Business Structure

After you've got your account up and running in the open now is the time to determine the appropriate legal designation for your company. (Also--before you pick which one you'll need to make sure that you've chosen which business you want to be referred to as. It will be required for the various documentation.)

The general rule is that there are three types of business structure to consider

Sole Proprietorship

Limited Liability Corporation (LLC)

A Subchapter S Corporation (S-Corp)

For a thorough understanding of the advantages and disadvantages of each, you should spend your time browsing the United States Small Business Administration site. Factors like location and the projected amount of revenue will play significant impact on impact of the choice Do your homework prior to the time.

Not All Structures Are Created Equal

The various businesses structures handle tax, fees and obligations in a different way.

In the case of a sole Proprietorship and you're a sole proprietor, you're personally responsible for any damage that might occur. If a customer sues the company (and is successful) you're personally liable for your assets like your automobile, your home etc.--may be in risk. In the same way, if a Sole Proprietorship borrows money from the bank, and then you fail in a repayment the personal assets of your business are in danger.

If you decide to form an LLC, it'll give you a liability-free shell (meaning the personal assets are protected from damage) However, it will also require additional fees and tax. The tax rates for the two Sole Proprietorships and LLCs pass through your individual income tax return.

S-Corps however, on the contrary they are enterprises which are completely independent of their proprietors. Similar to LLCs S-Corps safeguard you against liability, however they are different in that they remain in operation for the duration of time. Solo Proprietorships and LLCs need to be shut down if the proprietor dies or leaves the company. S-Corps have even greater paperwork and accounting (which obviously means more charges as well as a host of other issues) however, they provide an added level of legitimacy.

Naturally, you need to research this issue, but in the event that you're not convinced after completing your investigation, speak to an accountant or lawyer who will provide suggestions on the best option for your particular situation. Consider discussing the amount you believe you'll earn as well as what your potential exposure to liability could be. (Admittedly freelancers working in the field of e-Learning have less risk than say the construction industry, but in the case of industries which are heavily regulated with compliance standards You're still subject to an element of risk as well as danger.)

License and Registration, Please

If you're considering the type of organization structure you choose Be sure to be conscious of the licensing and fees in the area you're operating. Certain states may require at least one license which you must purchase in order in order to run your business legally dependent on your kind of business you are operating and where you're located. In my state of Oregon when you create an LLC it is legally required to pay multiple annual charges: a company registration cost of $100, the city's business license fee of $75and tax for the local transit authorities, TriMet. If you're unsure of the type of license for your business you'll require get started researching. Do not hesitate to talk with the advice of a Certified Public Accountant (CPA)!

3. The Tax Man Cometh

The last thing to mention is that when you're establishing your online e-learning business as a freelancer it is important to be informed of all taxes that apply to your business.

One thing you must learn about tax laws as freelancers is that they'll have to pay quarterly tax. That means every quarter, you'll be required send money to the IRS which is equal to 25% of your annual total tax amount due. Tax payments for the quarter are due in the months of April, June, September and January of the coming year.

However, these dates may change depending on the time of year, so be sure to do your homework prior to submitting your tax payments.

In Oregon in the state of Oregon, I'm obliged to pay state and federal taxes each three months. The taxes I pay during the year will be added up when I file my tax returns for the year. In addition, if I do not pay my quarterly tax then I'm subject to interest penalty, which could affect my financial situation!

In order to ease the burden that comes with quarterly tax obligations It is recommended that you set aside a amount of your earnings each time you are paid by your clients. It can be a bit complicated. As freelancers, your first biggest question to ask is, "How do I estimate my taxes if I get paid sporadically and inconsistently?" The good news is that the IRS provides an estimated tax worksheet that can assist you in making accurate estimates. Or, you could always consult together with your CPA for a more accurate estimation.

Don't Forget Self-Employment Tax!

As well as taxes on income, you'll be responsible for the payment of Social Security and Medicare taxes (a.k.a. "Self-Employment Tax"). If you worked previously in a firm, it's likely that you paid 6.6% in Social Security and 1.5% for Medicare, and your employer was contributing the same amount in your name. When you freelance, you're accountable for the whole amount, which is around 15 15%. It is essential to account Self-Employment Tax in the course of managing your business because these taxes will form an element of your tax return.

Where to Start

It's true that some of the things might seem to be a bit tedious, but the proper setup of your business is essential to the success of your freelancer working in the field of e-Learning.

If you're feeling confused You can start beginning with the basics, before getting to the finer details.

1. Pick a name for your company.

2. Create an account at a bank that you will only use for your company.

3. Determine if you would like to incorporate as an Sole Proprietor, LLC, or S-Corp firm and fill in all the necessary documents.

4. Determine the first percentage portion of the revenue that you'd like to reserve to pay taxes. (You could always alter your mind later but the earlier you begin saving money for tax purposes more efficiently.)

Keep in mind: The more time you spend at the beginning to your adventure, the better you'll be able to dedicate your time working on the thing that you're passionate about:

creating compelling online learning material.

Chapter 12: 4 Critical Things To Track

If you've noticed it that a major element of being successful freelancer is being organized If you're the boss, there's lots of work to keep the business running, which is stressful. But the good news is that by establishing several tracking systems as well as basic habits, you'll be able to reduce the amount of time that your business demands, which means you can concentrate on creating online learning materials.

Now let's talk about the details! In my opinion, these are four of the most crucial items you'll have to keep track of in your job as a freelance designer of e-Learning.

Revenue

Although it may seem like the obvious thing to track how much money is that is coming in, the key element of keeping a keen watch on your earnings is to do it frequently. As an example, I would suggest making a habit of recording each payment immediately upon receipt, because the longer you delay longer, the more likely you will encounter problems in the future.

For income, it is about making use of software to track every payment you get. The QuickBooks program, YNAB (You Need A Budget), Microsoft Excel, and Google Sheets are excellent instruments for tracking this. Make sure you test several options because much of the decision depends on what tool is the easiest for you to utilize and is one you feel at ease using on a daily basis. As your company grows as you expand, you are able to update to a more efficient program.

Alongside the revenue tracking software You'll need ensure that you keep in mind the invoices that you send to your clients. In the event that you track invoices, you'll be able compare your owed amount to the cash that's coming from. I suggest establishing the same time every week to send invoices. Be sure that each invoice contains important information such as your client's name, date, the full outline of your deliverable(s) and the expected conditions for payment (for instance, if your terms want to pay within 30 days, write "net 30" on the invoice).

The most difficult part of doing this is making it a routine, and any action you can take to maintain your discipline can be helpful. The past few times, I've set aside the time every Friday on my calendar to track earnings, in order to make sure that I'm making the time to do it, and make the time into my schedule.

Expenses

Tracking expenses can be difficult as it demands meticulous and focused. One thing you must remember is that each expense you keep track of will help you save cash in the end however, every expense that not tracked will result in a charge. As tax time approaches and you'll have the ability subtract your expenses from your tax liability, therefore be cognizant of each dollar that you're investing in the growth of your company. Most of the expenses I incur of my business include:

Domain registration and hosting charges

Internet connection bills

Mobile phone bill

Subscription fees for software

Office equipment

Legal and professional costs

Business lunches

In keeping track of receipts, you're keeping a record of the investment you've made into your company, which means your total may be less than that what you and the IRS is able to consider your income tax deductible. It's a given necessity of tracking the receipts, bills and payment is an arduous task therefore, make sure that you're taking care of it when you can. As an example, I've been into the habit of making a photo of my receipts and transferring them onto DropBox. DropBox cloud storage the moment I receive them.

Like tracking revenues and expenses, the hardest thing about spending tracking is learning how to do it, and staying in the habit on a regular schedule. It's not much worse than coming close to tax deadline and having to go through a whole calendar year's worth of your own reluctance!

Cash Flow

When you've got a solid system to track the amount of revenue you earn and expenses You'll be able to track both of them together and accurately assess the flow of cash. The flow of cash is the chance to monitor the amount of money flowing into and out of your business and to decide if you're earning profits or losing money in a specific amount of time. As an example, at the close of every month I look over my cash flow in order to take decisions on both aspects of the equation. Sometimes, it's an opportunity to remind me to ensure that my expenditures are in check or else it's an incentive to begin reaching for clients who have overdue payment due.

Small and freelance enterprises start with greater expenditures than income it's perfectly normal you need money for making money. Hence, you must begin with investing in essential tools to allow the ability to collaborate with clients. The goal to monitor cash flow isn't to ensure you're making an income every month -- you probably likely won't but you most likely experience good and bad ones, but rather to provide you a long-term view in order to make smart decisions regarding money.

Information on cash flows is beneficial in planning your financial goals, since you're not just keeping track of the financial consequences of events that occurred (like clients' payments or costs) but also taking into account data about future financial events. In the example above, if realize that your website's annual hosting charges will come due in 2 months the cash flow could reveal the effect the fees impact your earnings. In the same way, understanding how much you're planning to earn next month can aid in determining whether your month is going to make money or not.

One of the most crucial aspects to monitoring your cash flow is to anticipate emergency situations and financial issues. If, for instance, you know that you'll be short of funds to cover your current expenses for three months, keeping track of the flow of cash can provide the business an early signal that it will be required to make a decision. We hope you don't have to face such a situation however monitoring the flow of cash could be the most important factor in helping the business to thrive. (In the second volume of this collection, I'll discuss ways you can set up an sales pipeline that is a great way to track how soon you're likely to get funds.)

Also, as I've mentioned before that it's essential to keep your company's finances and personal accounts for financials separate. The tracking of your own personal money flow is almost impossible as you must separate the personal transaction from company transaction.

Goals

In the end, you must keep track of your professional and personal goals in a regular manner. It's quite easy to become distracted by the demands of work (and the endless accounting you must perform) And often the first thing freelancers forget to track is their personal progress and their personal development.

Take the time to reflect on your progress. What progress have you made towards your short-term or medium- the long-term objectives? What could require a renewed commitment? If you're not getting the outcomes you want How can be made to return to the path you want?

It Gets Easier, I Promise

In all honesty the process of tracking isn't my preferred part working as an independent freelancer. Monitoring expenses, revenues in cash flow and objectives means having to deal with a lot of details all of the time and the list never stops. Although it is a hassle after you've developed the techniques and habits that you've learned, it's a tiny part of work as a professional which will transform from an overwhelming and daunting list of tasks to a set of smaller activities that can help in the growth of your enterprise.

The Mantras of Tracking

In order to help me get past the monotony of all the work I need to complete as a freelancer I frequently have to keep myself in mind of certain items over and over again. Those reminders have become"tracking mantras. "tracking mantras":

The closer I keep track of my finances and track my spending, the more I can keep.

I commit some time for tracking, so that I have longer creating.

If I don't keep track of my progress toward my objectives, I'll not ever reach them.

When I keep these thoughts within my mind to keep my enthusiasm, and it makes it more easy to work through my daily tasks.

When you've completed the tracking exercises you've created Be sure to congratulate you on your back. keep in mind that, by doing this, you're making yourself more likely for success!

When your freelance company expands, you might discover that you are able to devote more and less time to complete the tracking of your activities. It's a good thing, since you would like to see your business grow! However, it's not easy to be involved in numerous details when your list of clients grows. When you get to a point that you're unable to keep a close focus on the finances of your company as you'd like to, you may need to consider the next stage of your career as a freelancer: getting professional assistance to manage your freelance income.

Chapter 13: When Should You Hire A Bookkeeper Or A Cpa?

In the beginning, when I began freelancing at the time, I was doing all my accounting and financial management by myself. While I didn't make much income, I was able to establish an organized system to track the invoices, expenses and payment--I had folders for each of them, and would review them for hours every month as well as on a on a quarterly basis. I was convinced that it was the best method of handling things since I wasn't looking to invest in an accountant and believed in my capabilities.

But what I didn't anticipate what I didn't expect was how long I spent tracking my finances on my own, and also how challenging (and tedious) it was to take my the time to make sure I had prepared my tax returns precisely. In the end, I engaged an accountant and Bookkeeper. Certified Public Accountant (CPA) however, despite the addition the cost of my services I've learned that I'm more secure financially when working with experts who handle my company accounts.

For this particular chapter I'll discuss the best time and method to take the decision to seek assistance with your financials.

The Case for Hiring an Accountant or Bookkeeper

It took me time to adjust my mind to the thought of hiring a financial expert. The business I was running was still in its beginnings, and I did not have any cash coming in, but I was very proud for the organized person I had developed. My mind was that I really didn't need any! However, as time passed some things came to mind to me:

I noticed that I spent an excessive amount of time my financial record. I wanted to spend more time growing my company-- marketing myself, locating new clients, building my portfolio -- but I was spending time each week by managing my cash flow.

I disliked doing accounting and financial issues, just like a lot of creative professionals. The longer I sat looking at spreadsheets and making summaries as I got older, the more I saw myself unable to do the tasks I set out to accomplish initially.

I was unable to get rid of the thought I didn't have a good grasp of tax law--and the annual revisions to the laws behind. Did I count all the correct expenses? Did I not pay attention to new legislation which could put me in legal troubles?

As I thought about it on it, the more I realized that I'd need to hire an expert. Once I had my only concern left to answer was "Why didn't I do this sooner?"

Bookkeeping vs. Accounting

Before you search the Internet for a professional to assist you in the management of your finances, it's crucial to be aware of the distinctions between accountants and bookkeepers.

Bookkeepers gather and collate the entirety of your company's financial records, and ensure that every transaction is documented and sorted. They provide a great deal of worth by identifying what information is the most crucial, as well as performing the difficult task to manage each transactions. For example, if you think you're planning an excursion to the wilderness the bookkeeper is your guide to inform you what to bring to ensure you're ready.

Accounting professionals, on the other on the other hand, evaluate your company's financial condition and offer direction and advice for your business They're commonly known as GAAP-ers due to their adherence to "Generally Accepted Accounting Principles." Recalling our camping analogy: while the bookkeeper will tell you what to take with you, an accountant on your side is similar to having an experienced forest ranger to assist you in using the items you have packed, and to ensure your entire camping experience goes without a hitch.

Accounting and bookkeepers usually collaborate often, and it's not unheard of to find skilled bookkeepers become accountants. There are certifications for both positions and are relevant in the case of accountants. A Certified Public Accountant (CPA) is able to file taxes on behalf of yourself and act as your representative when you face the IRS tax audit. A accountant who is not certified cannot perform either of these tasks.

Of course, CPAs have to keep updated with the latest tax legislation This means that they're equipped with the expertise to assist you make the most of every penny.